GET *REAL!*

A *REAL* look at Interpreting

Samantha Terzis CI/CT/ASLTA

GET REAL!

Copyright © 2013 by Samantha Terzis

ISBN 978-1491031261

Dedicated to:

<u>Hollis Greathouse</u>

Who warred for us endlessly in his wheelchair, and left a tremendous hole in our hearts when he left this earth.

Table of Contents

DISCLAIMER

There are thousands of perspectives and opinions about every aspect of the field of interpreting. I don't claim to know everything about the field. I don't claim to have all the answers. I definitely do not claim to be perfect. I know a few of the philosophies in this book might raise an eyebrow or scrunch a brow, but so much of what you will find on these pages are contemplations from the heart, thoughts often only whispered behind closed doors, or mentioned as backs are turned. Although not shouted from the rooftops, these issues are pervasive in the minds of so many in the field. This book is a collection of ideas, opinions, and stories which I hope will be challenging, inspiring, and truthful. This book is earthy, sarcastic, eclectic, and comical. It isn't meant for every reader. Some may want to resist the words within. Inside, many will finally find peace and solace. If you do choose to join me on this journey, please do so with an open mind and an open heart.

Preface

WHO SHOULD BUY THIS BOOK?

If you are an ITP student, buy this book! Read it! Study it! Take notes! This book is packed with things I wish I had known.

If you are a professional interpreter and you have found yourself at times tired, overwhelmed, confused, even alone, and sadly, imperfect, THIS BOOK IS FOR YOU!

Who should *not* buy this book? If you feel like a complete success, this book isn't for you. If you feel like you are the model for other interpreters, this book isn't for you. If you are quick to defend yourself and are not interested in suggestions for change, this book isn't for you. If you feel that the field is perfect as is, PUT IT DOWN NOW! This book isn't for you.

This book is about real people, in real situations, trying to fulfill sometimes unreal expectations under very difficult circumstances. This book says, "Hey! We are all in this together!" This book emphasizes that interpreters generally have room to grow. It targets the fact that people in the field have been diverted into some perspectives that may need a bit of tweaking. This book is very blunt and very honest. It says we can do more, be more, and expect more of ourselves and our field. It acknowledges our failings and reminds us to embrace our humanity and learn to work with the package we have been given. This book is poignant, and at times painful, but if you let it, it will challenge you and help you grow. You will laugh, you might shed a tear, and hopefully, you will leave this book feeling empowered, inspired, and blessed.

Introduction

Hi. My name is Sam. I am a real person. I live and breathe like the rest of you. I have hopes and dreams and desires and fears. I look at life through the eyes of my own personal history, my own belief systems, and my own experiences. I love animals. I love chocolate... maybe a little too much. I love Star Trek (I can't believe I confess that now!). I love people. I love God. I am a person. Oh, yeah... and I am a sign language interpreter.

After 23 years of interpreting, a million songs glossed (well, maybe not that many), countless jobs, and now decades of teaching, I have come to realize one very powerful truth: interpreting is hard. No, let's be even more honest, it's *REALLY* hard. I didn't wake up this morning and know I had finally "arrived" and am finally "great" at my job. I have not, and I am not. After decades on the job, there are still thousands of improvements I can make to my skill set. I am still growing, and I know I am not the only one.

As I have traveled the country and taught workshops, I have realized that there are scads of interpreters like me out there, real interpreters, with real emotions, real feelings, real problems, and who experience a real frustration regarding this ridiculous fantasy that interpreters are supposed to be "perfect". Recently, at a workshop, a beautiful interpreter said to me, "I am so glad you have the courage to say what no one else is saying." In that moment, she motivated me to do more than just speak on these topics. I knew it was time to write these truths on paper to hopefully encourage, arouse, and challenge individuals in our field to finally... GET REAL!

ONCE UPON A TIME

I was so cute and innocent when this all began. My story is pretty typical. I didn't start as a CODA (Child of a Deaf Adult). I didn't have Deaf friends. Like most Americans, I was just a Hearing kid, doing my Hearing thing, and none of it had anything to do with the Deaf. I was raised in the San Diego area, and my parents were big on camp when I was a kid. I think they just wanted to be rid of me for a few weeks. I was an insecure loner while traipsing through the mountains, but I loved the classes offered, and those classes soon changed my life. The camp allowed the students to pick the activities to attend and define portions of our daily schedule. I picked art, and swimming, and yes, I picked SIGN LANGUAGE.

We went into a small class, and there we sat down and learned to sign a song which would later be performed for the entire camp. All shyness and insecurity vanished. I fell in love with signed music, and it only took minutes. I loved moving my hands into all those shapes. I loved putting those shapes to music, and never in a million years would I have thought those silly signed music classes would radically shape my entire future. Whoever came up with that idea at Camp Cherith in the Big Bear Mountains, THANK YOU! I love the course of my life, and it all began with you.

Signing classes at camp led to signing classes at church a few years later. At the age of 15, I was in an awkward time of my life where my lack of self-esteem was now reeling uncontrollably. At that point, I didn't have a clue that it was possible to have any form of talent. I just thought sign language was pretty, so I sat down, and mustered up the courage to learn it. I enrolled in a basic course. I walked in scared, but excited about the future. The teacher pulled out a big yellow book and began to teach us. (I know some of you just grimaced.) I picked up the syntax and lexicon rapidly. People were asking me for advice and tutoring outside of class. *ME*? Odd. One day, months into the class, after countless requests for help from fellow classmates, I thought, "Why do they ask *ME*? Am I good at this?" I was, and it was a shocking revelation. I had never been skilled at anything. I was dumbfounded. That revelation motivated me to work exceptionally hard and become fluent in... you guessed it... SEE SIGN! (For you younglings, that's Signing Exact English.) The problem was I lived in California where they consider burning you in effigy for using SEE. Oops!

Straight out of high school, I met my first Deaf person. One of my best friends, Penny, was getting married. She had a Deaf friend whom she had, of course, invited to her wedding with her "+1" in tow. I was a cute little parasol carrying bridesmaid. Pen had created a unique program booklet. In it, all of the bridesmaids were listed with attached bios. There it was in print... *Samantha plans to teach the Deaf.* I stood on stage and saw her Deaf friends looking down at that program and reading that story. Then, they looked up and I thought, "They know! Now I can't avoid these people." But one can try!

When the wedding was over they walked towards me; I ran away. They pursued me again; I ran away. We played this game of, "Dodge the Deaf People" for hours at the primary reception. I was home free. What I didn't know is that they would attend the second reception, held in the family home. There was no escape; I was trapped. I gave it my best shot though, and found numerous ways to slither pass the living room where that lovely Deaf couple was happily positioned on the couch. Penny knew. She cornered me and asked, "Have you met Rick and Mindy?" I said, "No" with a fabulous display of innocence. You would have been impressed. She was not. She yanked me over to them and introduced me with her voice and said, "She can sign." What she of course failed to mention in an appropriate disclaimer is that "She could sign SEE SIGN!" *(Insert dramatic music)*. It didn't go well. Mindy was willing to chat for a few minutes, but she was at a party with her friends. There were many conversations to be had. Rick, however, was in uncharted territory, stuck with a slew of Hearing people he did not know. Like most Deaf people immersed in Deaf Culture, speaking and reading lips were not his primary form of communication, and no one else at the party signed. That meant the only hope for conversation was with this SEE SIGNER! *(Insert SCREAM)* It almost makes you want to hug him doesn't it? So Rick, sweet Rick, wonderful Rick, sat there with the terrified SEE student and put up with what probably was the most torturous conversation of his life. While watching a replay of the wedding video, and in an attempt to dispel the tension, he bravely said, "Look, you are a TV Star." I was doing fine until we arrived at the word STAR, which he fingerspelled, and of course, I PANICKED! "Huh?" "S-T-A-R." "Huh?" "S...T...A...R." "HUH?" "S.............T.............A............R." I thought "S+T+A+R... That isn't a word!" This infamous interaction among Deaf Community members must have become memorable to some extent. Years later, I found his email address online and emailed him to thank him for his kindness so many years before. His response? "You are *CERTIFIED*?" Haha. Ok. It was a totally justified response. I know he didn't leave that party with an enormous amount of respect for my phenomenal skill set. I can almost guarantee he left with a migraine. His kindness, though, was an example to Deaf people around the U.S. Because of him, I didn't walk away from the field. Often, in my early years, after a rough interaction with a Deaf individual, I would think back to his kindness that day. I would think of how he negotiated my fear with such compassion and patience, how he tenderly supported me when I was a clueless and terrified young student, and it reminded me of the goodness that can exist in our consumers. The fact was I could sign well enough to understand the word "STAR," but my fear paralyzed me, as it has for many of you at one time or another. However, I dreamed of teaching the Deaf and wanted desperately to become skilled in the language. I was relatively fluent in SEE, but that was only the beginning of my journey. I enrolled in a collegiate ASL (American Sign Language) class at a local Jr. College... and so the development of my professional career began.

I think the instructor must have had some vibe that a SEE Signer was entering his holy domain. On day one, he proceeded to teach the class without his voice. The students were completely confused. I understood him perfectly. I had a strong grasp of SEE and I had survived my first Deaf encounter, so I was ready! Innocence, it's a beautiful thing... while it lasts. It didn't. A day or two into the class, the students had to communicate back to the instructor. Now keep in mind, I was, "Sweet Innocent Sam". I was a little Christian girl, straight out of Christian schools, living my little Christian life, and I had no idea that my instructor was EVIL! Ha. Well, he might have not been that bad, but he hated SEE Signers and I had no idea that I was about to get introduced to that hatred in a bold way.

It was time to practice. We went around the room signing sentences to the instructor. When it came to my turn, with my innocence and naivety firmly intact, I signed, "I (with an 'I') will (with a 'W') be (with a 'B')..." and it went downhill from there. Now I am 5' 1" tall. He was 6'+ bearded and relatively scary. He could sport facial expressions which would shake you to your core! He truly was a scary man, and knew it, even took pride in it. My error was innocent. He didn't seem to care, not even a little itsy bitsy teeny tiny bit. He walked straight up to me, loomed over me with his statuesque frame, got down in my face, and screamed in Sign language "STOP BASTARDIZING MY LANGUAGE!" He followed this proclamation of my unforgivable blunder with an onslaught of disparaging remarks and accusations. He was unhappy... and it showed. I mean, it *really* showed. When the class was over, and I was sufficiently crucified in front of the students, we all walked out, and one of the students looked at me and said, "I didn't understand a word he said, but he looked really mad." I responded, "I understood him fine. He *WAS* mad." Dang, was he mad. He liked drama, and I will say he could have won an Emmy that day. I almost left the field. Looking back, I think about how many lives around the world I have been able to touch, how many beautiful moments in the field I have had, and it all almost ended because of the hateful agenda of one man. I did learn something that day. SEE Sign was probably not the favorite form of communication among the California Deaf. I learned that lesson well, and it's a lesson I have never forgotten.

My original plan was to obtain my degree in Art, Theatre, and Interpreting, then follow it with a teaching credential from CSUN (Cal State Northridge). Since I am not writing this book as an Art/Theatre instructor at a residential high school for the Deaf, clearly things didn't work out as planned. Do they ever? Day after day, I found myself thrown into interpreting assignments. My vision of teaching was placed in my back pocket, and interpreting was where I stayed. Since my plan was never to interpret, I had no idea what the interpreting community would be like or how my life would morph in the field. I had no idea of the difficulties which would arise. I had no idea of the personal struggles I would face. I just wanted to sign. Sign language was pretty, and although my role as an interpreter would be quite different than my role as a Deaf educator, I hoped I could still make an impact on the paths I crossed along the way.

In a seemingly short amount of time, my interpreting career was under way. The bloom fell off the rose rather quickly when I realized how difficult the job was. I was in a generation of interpreters (ouch...

feeling old) that had never heard of the concept of mentoring, we had no significant resources, hardly any Sign language texts; we literally had almost nothing! We went in relatively cold and hoped for the best. That led to some good days, and some bad days, but it meant we had to have a lot of courage. I walked into this field with a halo and a bag of hopes and dreams, and since then, it's been a wild ride.

LIVING IN TERROR

I am not one of those interpreters who walked out of an ITP (Interpreting Training Program) feeling confident and ready to face the world. Honestly, I don't believe those types of interpreters exist. Even the ones I have met who appear confident have insecurities and are faking some of that confidence. CODAs are not void of fear and intimidation either. I have met CODAs who are terrified of voicing in front of their peers, scared they won't impress me during a job interview, or even leave the field because someone didn't think they were good enough to do the job. No matter the amount of community exposure or experience we have, none of us are immune to fear.

I have never been an incredibly confident person. I have a vast array of reasons for my insecurities which will inevitably find themselves documented in a book one day for your reading pleasure. However, today, let's skip over Sam's life drama and just state, "I had issues!" I can remember my first official interpreting assignment. I was hired to interpret at a church. Let me note, this was a dream job. The consumer was the nicest man on the planet with little to no expectations. The church gave me a printed version of the entire service word for word. It seriously could not have been a better position for an interpreter straight out of the starting gate. However, prepared or not, I walked into every service terrified. After this position, I was then hired to interpret in schools. I was terrified. A Deaf guy visited a family member on my college campus. Outside of his family bonding, he was being interviewed by a student for a class paper. Someone requested I voice the interview. A new interpreter providing 45 minutes of straight voicing? Terrified. I started getting hired for concerts. 5,000 people watching me interpret? Terrified. "Terrified" pretty much sums up the first 15 years of my interpreting career! I know I was an extreme case, but what so many young interpreters don't realize is that interpreters at all stages of their careers get scared. Granted, I might win some type of scaredy-cat award, but my experience is not entirely unique. My fear became so crippling at one point, every single time the phone rang with the potential for a freelancing job; I panicked. *EVERY TIME!*

A lot of interpreters are afraid of their assignments. Why? There are a number of reasons.

– The Lie of the Great Faux Pas –
"Mistakes Mean Permanent Job Loss"

First, there is this ridiculous notion which started in the '80's that if you make a mistake you will never work again. I suppose the theory was targeting the fallacious belief that somehow, a mysterious network of Deaf people would jump on their TTYs after every error and launch into a national campaign to end an interpreter's career. This is no exaggeration. I was told by a professor in my ITP program that if I made a mistake in California, people in New York would know the details of my interpreting blunder before my frizzy Greek head hit the pillow that night. Really? Sadly, this belief that a single error translates to lifetime job loss is absurd, but people have believed it. I did, and it was that belief which began my personal trek of terror. At least, it was a contributing factor.

Let's address this here and now. You *will* make mistakes and you *will* work again. I am sure there have been a few doozies interpreters have made on occasion which have eventually led to losing a job or several jobs, and I am sure that a few interpreters have developed a chronic bad reputation. I am not disregarding the fact that interpreting, like any job, if done improperly, can cause problems. However, that being said, it is an extremely rare event for an interpreter to have to leave the field after an interpreting snafu. At least in my 23 years in this field, I have never heard of it happening. So breathe! If this fear has been looming in your noggin, put it to rest and move on. You might foul up enough to make a few people mad, or even see a bit of gossip traipse about with your name attached, but time passes and rumors will subside. Do your job to the best of your ability and let those fears go.

– Distracted by Perspectives –
"I Don't Want to 'Look Stupid'"

What else causes us to live in terror? Interpreters don't want to "look stupid". The cold hard truth is that we all have some form of insecurities lurking inside of us, and those can grab a hold of our "fear of man" and wreak havoc on our minds when we find ourselves in the hot seat. I cannot begin to list the number of times in which I did a job and had to fight pervasive fears highlighting the mother of all my fears, "What will they think of me?" I have never met an interpreter who hasn't struggled with this at one time or another. We all have those moments.

Clinging to Truth

I have learned a couple of truths which can easily address these protracted fears.

Truth Number One: Most people are not sitting there with a mental note pad documenting your errors. Just last night I went to a job where I had to interpret for a sizable group of Deaf individuals. A few of my interpreters were also present. As the boss, I really don't want to look rough in front of my work family! I was in one of those "not so ideal" situations. I had just received the layout of the event. The job was to include a mix of speeches and music. The positioning was horrendous, there was no sound monitor, no hope of effectively hearing voices. There wasn't much about this job that made me think, "Oh, goody." The event started; my hands began to form words, and by the end of the night, I had a long mental list of things I knew I should have done differently. First, I body shifted left when right would have been better. Second, I clapped facing straight ahead even though I teach people to turn towards the stage when clapping to represent the crowd. Third, I didn't like the consistency of my mix of ASL/Contact (had a diverse crowd and was shooting for a balance). Fourth, I could go on, but I will refrain. When the event was over and I walked over to the Deaf to say goodbye, I had mentally documented my list of "Next time, Sam, you need to...'s." One of the participants looked at me and said, "You are a wonderful interpreter! So clear! Thank you so much for interpreting for us tonight." Did she not see that I turned left when right would have been better? Did she not see every error I made as clearly as I did? Then one of my interpreting staff members walked up to me and said, "You did great. I could hardly hear anything and you did far better than I could have." Was she high? Yikes! I hope not. She works for me. The truth was that although I was critically evaluating myself, they were not keeping copious notes on my array of "oopses". Was there a deep seeded need for my looming fears? Nope.

Truth Number Two: You are going to look stupid sometimes. Get over it. One time I was interpreting at a church. I can't remember the topic, but I remember having to represent the voice of approximately eight different characters in a story. Those eight body shifts were going great. I busted into my well defined set-up and moved left, right, left again. The comments got faster. I was on it. The pastor kept moving and I kept shifting. Every few seconds I had to change direction, then suddenly, I got tired. My coffee stimulated brain lacked the necessary extra espresso shot to manage this endless rat-race of shifts, and I got off track. I then realized I was off and tried to correct it. I did. That lasted for a minute, and then I snapped. I suddenly went to turn at the next comment and couldn't figure out where I had put anybody. I turned back and forth and half-shifted hoping to jog my memory, and in the end, I looked out at the Deaf who were far more interested in how I would handle this contorted speech over one ounce of content in the speech itself. I had nothing. **TILT!** I confess, I stepped out of my role for a moment (don't judge me), and I said, "I have no idea where I put anyone." The Deaf erupted in silent laughter momentarily. They got their awaited entertainment for the day. I erased my mental slate and started again. Yeah, I looked stupid for a moment. No one would blame me, mind you. My reputation was marred only momentarily but I recovered. It will happen, people! We are going to make mistakes. You *will* look stupid at some point so embrace your imperfection and move on.

One of our biggest problems is that we are scared to look stupid, or unskilled, or dare I say imperfect. We often perceive we are being critiqued every minute that we are on the job. We aren't! I honestly believe this type of fear is a tad self-centered. Why do I think people are contemplating *me* every minute? They are trying to just enjoy the *event*! I think as interpreters one of our biggest problems is that we just flat out need to get over ourselves. We can get so caught up in worrying about what other people think of us, that we miss the fact that they *aren't* thinking about us. I believe that self-obsession is a bit narcissistic and unprofessional, and sadly I have worked for many years marred by these perspectives. I have overcome a great deal, but I still have to work on my insecurities. I told you, I haven't arrived yet. I do know that I need to get over myself and just do my job every single time I sit in the hot seat. Maybe by the time I write my next book I will be there. Then again, maybe not, but one can hope.

I am sure someone out there stopped a second ago and thought "Well, clearly you don't know the interpreters in my area! They *ARE* critiquing me!" I know some of you have considered applying for a renaming of your city to "Egoville, U.S.A." I am not saying there aren't those interpreters out there who sit down with an agenda to watch other interpreters on duty, already armed with an onslaught of disparaging allegations which they can apply to your presentation at any moment. Have no fear, we will address those types of people later. Suffice it to say, those interpreters are not perfect either. None of us are! Don't let those people rule you or your thoughts. I am not a huge lover of Facebook, but something was posted there that made me stop and think. It said, "Don't let negative people rent space in your head." That is so true! If you encounter interpreters with an edgy feistiness, feel for them. If they can't look at you with a kind heart, they derive their harsh critiques from their own personal issues, their own anger, their own insecurities, even their own fears. It's sad, but it's very common. A good mentor always teaches and advises out of a heart of love. So, let go of your fears of critique. If not, this distraction will clog up your mind, and thus, your interpreting.

– Distracted by Concern –
"I Don't Want the Deaf to Look Bad"

And yet there is more which drives our worries! Interpreters don't want to make the Deaf look bad. It's true. Hearing people can misunderstand our errors as being errors made by the Deaf. I love interpreting foreign language classes, and one semester I was blessed to serve as an interpreter in a French class. To throw out my personal disclaimer, I grew up in San Diego. We generally focus on speaking Spanish out there, so my French was mediocre at best, and although watching the movie *French Kiss* over and over might assist with my French pronunciation on some level, it could not prepare me for the complication of speaking French in a classroom. One particular day the Deaf student fingerspelled something in French, and I voiced her correctly worded French statement (Note: I didn't say I voiced it well). The teacher heard what was said and proceeded to correct her on her pronunciation. In some ways that was a compliment. The teacher had forgotten I was in the class and felt so comfortable with an interpreter present that she saw me as truly being the direct voice of the student. Ah, warm interpreter fuzzy for Sam! However, the student had just *spelled* what she said in French, I was the one putting a voice to the language, and therefore the culpability for the incorrect accent was mine and mine alone. I stopped and indicated the fault was due to the ineptitude of "yours truly" and the student relished in "Sam getting busted" in French class. Problem solved, we moved on. Did I make the Deaf consumer look bad? Only momentarily. Was it an ideal situation? No. Did it permanently and irreparably damage her? No, not even close. One minute later, we were onto a different subject and life went on.

There are situations where an interpreter's inaccuracy can be a problem. We all know that is possible. There are a thousand scenarios I could invent or describe where a Deaf consumer could be or has been poorly served. What I am saying, though, is that most errors are redeemable. Ironically, the fear of making them, can, and in many cases, has, crippled interpreters on the job and caused problems which never would have existed. We need to do the job and do it to the best of our ability. Don't let this fear rule you. Remember 95+% of the time, your errors are not that big of a deal.

– Managing the Terror –

So what do we do when fear cripples us on a job? You have to address your self-talk. Did you say, "I can't do this"? That is a beeline for disaster. That statement is a self-fulfilling prophecy waiting to happen. Did you say, "I *can* do this"? That is also the beginning of a trek into the land of "uh oh". The fact is that the best thing any interpreter can do before walking on to a job is to say, "I am a professional. I am here to do my job professionally." That's it. Don't talk yourself into or out of success. Don't evaluate your success or failure while on the job. Avoid all forms of back-chatter. If you are in the middle of a successful interpretation, one fleeting yet permeating thought stating, "I am nailing this" can fashion an interpreting catastrophe five seconds later. If you are tanking, pondering your downward spiral just makes you spiral with greater momentum. If you have no expectations outside of being a professional, you are far more likely to handle yourself appropriately and effectively. When you make a mistake, correct it without the added self-deprecation. When you succeed, don't let your expectations influence the next thing you present. You simply do your job professionally. Doing your job perfectly isn't an option. That is the key to success on a job. Sadly, it took me numerous years to figure out this concept and how, prior to this revelation, I had not been placed in the loony bin was a flat out miracle.

– Personal Check Ins –

Someone who desperately wants to argue with this concept might say, "You have to evaluate your effectiveness and continually make minor adjustments to your interpreting while on the job." You are correct! That's a different issue all together. Presenting an interpretation and self-analyzing to correct small errors or improve upon your interpretation is absolutely necessary! There is a radical difference between contemplating "CL:A will work better than CL:C" vs "I can't do this! I am lost!" Interpreters find it critical to develop personal evaluation skills which can be accessed while on the job. This kind of interpretation adjustment is necessary and very valuable when producing a continually budding translation while on the job site. This, however, is never self-inflation or denunciation. It involves no expectations and no emotions; it is merely contextual tweaking which renders a more perfect production of the interpretation. Do it! But do it sans (without) emotion.

So far, men reading this chapter are likely facing utter confusion. Men, sometimes, can't relate to much of what was just discussed. Why? Let's call a spade a spade: men generally don't obsess like women do. I sometimes get a bit jealous of the male psyche (then of course I think of every aspect of the male psyche and I quickly refrain from that envy). In this scenario, single minded men who aren't driven by emotion are unquestionably better off than us multitasking emotion driven females. Guys... you have got it good. Relish in it.

– To the True Worry Warts –

Before we end this chapter, I want to address those interpreters truly paranoid to their core, those mentally and emotionally twisted interpreters out there... those PEOPLE LIKE ME! You may have heard the phrase, "Courage is not the absence of fear; it is the judgment that something else is more important than fear." – *Ambrose Redmoon*. There is a speaker named Joyce Meyer who said something that I have tucked away for interpreting jobs. She said, "Do it afraid." If you let your fears control you, you will never accomplish what you set out or even hope to do. So, fellow terror driven Terps, be courageous, face those fears, look in the mirror, decide to be a professional, dump the back-chatter, and go do that job to the best of your ability. I doubt I have ever taught a workshop, a college class, or worked an assignment where at some point I didn't have at least a brief moment of alarm rear its ugly head. In many cases, as we have established, I faced far more than a brief bout with nerves. Here is the truth though; I am still here 23 years later. I have survived. I have had to push through the dread and the panic and follow the philosophies listed in this chapter. I feel strongly there is someone reading this book that needs to hear this directly from me... DON'T GIVE UP! Do not stop interpreting. You can do this. You may have looked at yourself in the mirror and thought, "Why do I try?" You might have believed the lie, "I will never get better." Today might be hard, but your tomorrows will be filled with successes. I will see you there and we can celebrate our victories together.

TERZIS TIPS!

STIMULANTS ARE OUR FRIENDS

Never knock a good stimulant. I am definitely NOT advocating for illegal drug usage or the mishandling of prescription medication, but coffee is a gift from God. Tea is a blessing as well. We have a difficult job. We often cannot do our job as effectively if we don't have a little outside help. Vitamins! Herbal Supplements! CAFFEINE!

Sometimes, although I try to be health conscious and live sugar-free, a candy bar can save a rapidly deteriorating interpretation. Managing information in and information out at a fast pace is very difficult and there is no question that some of the unique and complicated subjects we have to translate are mind boggling in the Source Language. God help us when we have to analyze their meaning and present them in a

Target Language, often on no sleep, while we are PMSing, after we ran over a small animal on the way to a job, which happened because we received a frantic life altering text message in the car, which is illegal to read, but we read it anyway. So we have impossible information to translate, raging hormones, no sleep, illegal behaviors, the new status of "animal killer," and a thousand other problems in our head which we now have to manage at the same time that we are presenting our incredibly clear and accurate interpretation! Coffee helps. OK – supplements do too. Sleep if at all possible. And remember, never deny the power of a poisonous sugar filled candy bar in an energy deficient moment when your interpretation is heading South (just remember to eat it on a break). The important thing is to keep your mind sharp, your energy high, and to be an effective interpreter.

CAN'T AFFORD A HIT MAN?

I saw an email once that said, "Forward this if someone is alive today because you couldn't afford a hit man." I laughed until I cried, and then forwarded it to all my friends. I know people who have inspired the need for hit man fundraising campaigns. I have worked with some of those people. I see those people at national conventions. If you have no idea what I am talking about you likely *ARE* one of those people, so go ahead and skip to the next chapter.

The fact is there are some pretty scary interpreters in America today. Let's define a few of the gems we encounter on a regular basis in the field.

FRUSTRATING INTERPRETER #1
THE EGOTISTICAL INTERPRETER

Let's just get this topic out of the way. My goodness, some interpreters think you are standing on holy ground when you are in their presence. Have you ever met those people? I wonder what they think when they wake up every day and stare into their mirrors.

"CHAMP ME!" I am a trouble maker. Have you picked up on that yet? I was so clueless when I was young, but as an adult, I don't know, I just love to "stir the pot" a little. I confess, I want to walk up to those people when I see them on a job or at a conference and fall to my knees and bow down face to the floor. Ha! I wonder how they would react. I sometimes want to use my Art degree to create a snazzy looking sign which reads "I need to get over myself" and stick it to their backs as I walk by them. I don't perceive that as going over well, so I have refrained. Good for me. I just wish those interpreters would realize they are not little mini-gods and their arrogance is doing more harm than good.

– The Ones Who Inspire –

I see this arrogance running rampant all over the country. I teach workshops from coast to coast and I have met some of the most talented people in the industry. And you know what? There is one primary consistency among the great interpreters of America: they don't perceive themselves as "great". For example: Bob. A lot of you know Bob. He may not be a "mini-god" but he is one talented dude. He can voice for anyone, anywhere, any time and do it incredibly well. You become so entranced by his voicing that you wouldn't notice a mistake if one was flashed on a neon sign. I have seen CODAs terrified to work with him because he is so skilled. I have seen interpreters across America fawn over him. Bob's "the bomb," and he doesn't know it (or he fakes humility well when I am around). I would bet if you sit down with Bob he could mention 50 mistakes he made in the last week. He isn't perfect, but he is dang good, and honestly, I believe his humility is part of what defines his greatness.

Then there is Marie. She has been in the field longer than most of us have been alive, and Marie is a phenomenal voicer. She sits down for a two hour voicing gig in front of 1000 people like she had just been requested to read a "See Jane Run" book to a four year old at bedtime. Nothing fazes her. She is a rock and an incredible interpreter. Marie isn't perfect. Marie knows it, yet Marie is one of the most respected interpreters in the country, and she is anything but egotistical on a job. I am not saying she isn't opinionated or feisty, she is, but when I compliment her, she acts like it's nothing and moves on. She is great and part of her greatness is defined by her humility.

– Those Less Inspirational –

Then there are other interpreters. *THOSE* interpreters, as I call them. The ones we meet or work with who view their skills as the god-like example of "what to do". These are the interpreters who take over a job with disregard to others not because they are the lead interpreter, but because *THEY* know what to do. They are overzealous evaluators, the "I know what I am doing" people, the "I don't need your help" people, the "It's all about *ME*" people. These interpreters are unteachable, inconsiderate, and their level of value is defined by their self-perception of perfection. These interpreters don't care about their teams, they don't care about their consumers, not really; they solely care about themselves. They take narcissism to a whole new level, and honestly, I confess that I hate working with them or having to deal with them at my workshops. Wouldn't it be cool if we had an ego-meter? That way when we go to a job, we could scan our team interpreter and if the indicator on the ego-meter rapidly moves into the red, reads "Warning!" and buzzers or flashing lights start going off, we could run screaming from the building then call for a different team. Yep, that would be nice. If only...

Gate Communications has held a workshops in a well-known part of the country, an area which houses a large number of interpreters. We have actually taught three workshops in that particular state, and two of the three were inundated with outrageous egotism. I had never seen anything like it, and no other area of the country has compared (thank God). What happened, you say? It was loads of fun. (Please recognize the sarcasm of *THAT* statement.) I would present information, and a number of superior ego-driven interpreters, uninterested in what I was teaching, would argue. They didn't ask questions, or make suggestions, or mention alternative ideas, oh no, that would have been welcomed. Nope, these people came solely to argue. I am sure they had their agenda well established before they ever entered the building, and arguing was on the top of the list, right above complaining, which was right above patting themselves on the back. So argue they must, and they did. Argue, **Argue**... *ARGUE!* I would prove a concept through media (e.g.: Deaf consumer opinions on tape, or popular movies showing a similar and obviously effective philosophy). They would argue. I would provide ear plugs and offer them the chance to experience the theories from a Deaf perspective, which makes the most effective theory quite obvious. They would argue. We invited their local Deaf Community to evaluate the participants and talk about their personal preferences. Their own Community members stood up and said "She is right! That is what we want!" How did they respond? You guessed it, they argued. I concede their arguing with me was exhausting, but watching as they ignored the valiantly professed preferences of their very own consumers? That felt nearly unforgiveable. Before the end of those workshops, I felt strongly that a lobotomy would have been more fun and productive than attempting to educate interpreters in that state. During our last workshop in that general locale, after the eighth time I had attempted to pass along what seemed to be a repeatedly validated truth, and after that truth was again brazenly discounted, I realized a few things about the feisty ruckus causing crowd that was before me: a) they had pre-established unalterable opinions b) they literally didn't care one iota about what I was saying, they only cared about re-emphasizing their pre-established unalterable opinions and c) they didn't truly care about the opinions of their consumers when those opinions contradicted their pre-established unalterable opinions. Those workshops were memorable, very *very* memorable, and sadly, it happened in my absolute favorite part of the country. I could go on. We witnessed well known highly skilled interpreters sit down and refuse to participate when they weren't being called out by the Deaf evaluators as the iconic examples of skillful Performance Interpreting. We saw an interpreter try to refute everything I was saying using Google searches, then added to the dissenting drama by rallying his co-workers into a subtle revolt against me while I was speaking! Someone! Find me an eye-roll! The stories are endless but the fact is that every story was fueled by one thing... *EGOTISM.* The result? In spite of the fact we made great friends there, had some wonderful attendees in workshops, even met some of our BSL NASHVILLE family members at those very workshops, Gate decided, for a time, to table all requests for additional workshops in that state. It was a self-preservation tactic. Since then, our friends and interpreting family from the area have convinced us to open our doors once again to the beautiful state of (*not tellin'*), but we have done so with trepidation.

Did anyone benefit from their actions? No. They caused division, dissent, irritation, and frustration. Although the arguers did not notice the responses of the crowd, often around them were sighs of exhaustion, eye rolls, scowls, signed remarks of disapproval, or my personal favorite, one Terp throwing his head and arms on the desk in total defeat when one of those skilled terps argued for the umpteenth time. That moment was priceless as an instructor, and especially as an instructor equally drained by the arguing. High five dude! You always make me giggle when I think of you.

– Wreaking Havoc –

How does "ego" wreak havoc on the field? First "wreaking" method: Egotistical interpreters **create division, not unity**. It's hard to work with a team interpreter who is not a team player. Have you ever been on a job with an arrogant interpreter? I have. Their presence turns into a divisive element causing segregation between teams, as well as between interpreter and consumers. They cause mayhem with their attitudes and their actions. Is that ever what an interpreter should do? Interpreters by their very nature are supposed to offer unity and equality, so that division is in direct conflict with the foundational tenets of the field, yet for many interpreters, it is the choice they make. That discordant interaction is manifested in their words, their body language, their facial expressions, their choices, their requests, their demands, and their reactions. You all have seen it (and I say this in love, if you haven't, you are probably the one doing it). You might see it when they arrive on an assignment and take over with complete disregard to the feelings of the other interpreter or the professionalism of their choices along the way. You might come face to face with a bold illustration of this fun personality characteristic when you sit in the hot seat and they refuse to feed you information. I *love* when that happens. You might not even have to wait for your interpreting to begin. Their delightful conjugation of egotism can be marked in a mere "Hello," which when accompanied by their welcoming facial expression and body language, becomes apparent to even an amateur psychologist as meaning, "Stay the heck away from me." Yep, those interpreters are fun and their divisive nature is always a "plus" isn't it? (Note the sarcasm.)

The second havoc inspiring issue: Egotistical interpreters are **unteachable,** and therefore, their skills often become stagnate. There are no perfect interpreters. Let me say it again, because this concept needs to pierce every terp brain out there. *THERE ARE NO PERFECT INTERPRETERS!* We all have room to grow, and that growth is bred out of evaluation. Interpreters unwilling to receive constructive criticism end up with a flatlining skillset. I see this all the time in every area of interpreting, but one overlooked and surprising field of note is in the educational sector. Interpreters get into educational interpreting positions and as years go on, they become very comfortable with their careers. In the end, they feel no improvement or change is needed because of their years of experience, and lack of student complaint. Sadly, many of these interpreters have long since stopped their career progression and are stuck years down the road with no skill advancement. I was in the educational sector for many years, and I know from personal experience how easy it is to get comfy in that environment. I had to catch myself. In my comfort, I would start to make choices where I would settle for something which I would have not normally accepted. Ironically, what interpreters often don't realize, is that deep inside that undisturbed mindset, one can house a quiet stubbornness, and dare I say, an ego. People often don't acknowledge its existence in that setting, but it's there. Often, the subtle intractable perspectives of educational interpreters can manifest in comments like: "Things are fine," "The kids understand me and I understand them," "I have been doing this forever; I know what I am doing." What they mean is "I am comfortable, and I don't want to change." Why? Doesn't it serve your consumers and your teams if your skills continuously mature? How can alteration, enhancement, and progression ever be bad? I worked in schools for nearly a decade. I confess, I felt pretty darn secure by the time I left. When I started to settle in too much, I would stop myself and intentionally seek change. Thank God where I ended up was not where I started. I saw most days as an opportunity to grow, and I made that a part of my personal resolve. It wasn't comfortable, but it was important and I hope the interpreter I was when I left the educational sector showed marked improvement over the interpreter I was when I began. Oh, and to all my students who are now adults with families, I apologize for every faux pas. I know there must have been plenty.

Is it just the educational interpreters who have a struggle in this area? Clearly that is *NOT* the case. Interpreters in the freelance world are equally as stubborn and sometimes even worse. (Ok, ok! Put down the blow torch. I am not done yet. If you made the mistake of reading this chapter, just stick it out.) Traditionally, the longer an interpreter has been in the field, the more unwilling to receive feedback they become. Let me stop and just say, willingness to receive feedback is not a license for the individual *giving* feedback to throw harsh criticism at an interpreter. That is ironically founded in, you guessed it, egotism. I also don't believe comments should be dispelled at inappropriate times. Additionally, I don't presume interpreters are well served by getting feedback every time we sit in the chair. I do believe, however, that on occasion, asking a team interpreter or consumer to offer their thoughts is beneficial. Working with a mentor is equally beneficial. That feedback makes a true impact and we can use it to solidify or enhance our skills. I have heard one very consistent statement from Deaf Consumers across the U.S., "Interpreters don't want feedback." It doesn't matter what area of the country you live in, I can guarantee that a Deaf Consumer there thinks that same thing. I have seen it time and time again. Many Deaf Consumers are intimidated by egotistical interpreters, so much so, that I practically have to beg them to give feedback at our workshops. Clearly these terps have made quite an impression in their particular areas, and their choices have limited their career growth in addition to their relationships with their teams and consumers.

The wreak continues with number three (Note: there is a lot of "wreaking" going on): Egotistical interpreters are like a **dark cloud**. Now, I am not talking about a looming eerie haze. Egos start as a thunderstorm and can reach the equivalent of an EF5 tornado once a good dose of narcissism is invested. It's incredible how fast a positive, uplifted interpreter can at one moment be unsuspectingly sitting on his/her happy silver lining, only to be knocked off and forced to career head first toward the earth, all by the hands of an interpreter with an attitude. The hard core truth is that egos breed an atmosphere of tension, apprehension, and heaviness, plus they cause insecurity, uncertainty, and doubt from those working in close proximity. The best part of this is that egotistical interpreters have no idea the distress their presence causes. They are often determined to believe that they are just "doing their job," while the rest of us are trying to run for cover from the storm which looms around us.

Let's keep on wreaking havoc with number four: Interpreters can influence an environment in either positive or negative ways. (Personally, I think positive should win over negative, but that's just my personal preference.) Egotistical interpreters can **create drama** on a job leaving a negative imprint on an assignment. What kind of drama, you say? If you have to ask, you might not have worked with one of these gems. I have seen egotistical interpreters railroad the employees on a job, make inconsiderate demands, threaten their onsite contacts, then, in a final display of professionalism, follow it up by griping to their consumers. I have seen them walk into an assignment like a bulldozer and God help anyone who gets in their way! Yep. Treasures are they. (My Yoda reference.)

Fifth and final method of "havoc wreaking": Egotistical interpreters **cannot hide their egotism** during their interpretation. Egotists usually sit in their interpreting seat budding with varying degrees of inspiring personality traits, any of which could be pride, arrogance, over-confidence, irreverence, irritation, inconsideration, bitterness, condescension, etc. It is impossible to lift one's hands, begin interpreting, and leave those characteristics behind. The fact is that the influence of those inward issues becomes an outward misrepresentation of the voice of the consumer. That egotism, whether intentional or not, will often inappropriately and negatively influence an interpretation.

This truth has affected me personally as of late. For the last four years, I have been traveling the country and speaking at workshops where sign language interpreters have been used to tackle my fast paced verbal instruction. I sometimes SimCom a workshop, but usually I get a growl or two when I do because I don't hold still. What can I say? I am well caffeinated. (Some spirited interpreter who is ready to burn me in effigy after this chapter is saying, "Well, you should teach in ASL!" FYI, I do on occasion, but as most of my workshops are Performance related, speech works better for the information I cover.) At these workshops, the hosts often provide for me their best interpreters. I frequently hear how "so-and-so" is the most amazing interpreter in the area, and I will just love him/her. Within five minutes, my impending love relationship has usually waned, and I am begging God for the interpreter to stop misrepresenting me. Why? EGO! As I stand in front of the on looking crowd, cracking my stupid jokes (and if you have attended my workshops, you know there is no lack of those), presenting far too much info for the allotted time frame, I maintain a hope that the Deaf attendees at my workshops will get a solid dose of "Sam" before all is said and done. When I get an egotistical interpreter, it doesn't happen... ever. I am easy going, friendly, casual; it's a specific teaching style I have purposely chosen. Normally, these interpreters are standing erect, chin up, egos blazing, and no "Crazy Sam" can be found anywhere in their presentation. That's not how I stand. That's not how I look. That's not how I interact with the crowd, and that's a misrepresentation of "me". My goal at every workshop is to show how Certified Interpreters can be *REAL*, human, supportive, loving, and in my case, easily distracted, loud, and crazy. (People who know me well just said to themselves, "Wow, she just nailed that description.") I hate when I am told, "She really didn't represent you well." Argh! I am the consumer too! I want to be represented as *ME* just like a Deaf consumer wants his/her voice properly represented. In some cases, that even has a financial impact, as the people holding the purse strings are sometimes the Deaf individuals watching the interpreter! They miss my erratic jokes, they miss my friendliness, they miss my teaching style, all of which people say engages them in my workshops. Why would they be interested in asking me back? I confess, it's frustrating to me as a speaker, so I can imagine that it is infinitely more frustrating to the Deaf consumers who watch these misrepresentations daily.

You might say, "Does it *really* affect the Deaf?" Here's a story to define this for you skeptics. One day, years ago a local educational interpreter was on a job. She had plans to leave work for a period of time, and her student begged her not to take off even for a day. Why, you ask? Did you ask that? Well, if you didn't I am telling you anyway. The Deaf student knew the local agency which serviced that particular school district would send a specific interpreter, and that interpreter scared her. Why? Her EGO! I will stop and give credit where credit is due. That interpreter is one of the most certified interpreters in her state. I know her, although not well, but I get the sense she wants to be great at her job. She has good intentions. I can see behind the mask of her ego. The student could not. The interpreter has a business card full of letters after her name, but the fact is she didn't present herself as a supportive, kind, and loving professional woman. She looked irritated, exhausted, uninterested, and yes, egotistical. Her presentation scared the student. The regularly assigned interpreter was far less skilled, far less experienced and far less professional compared to the alternative token RID Certified Terp, but the student wanted the uncertified smiley interpreter, *not* the interpreter with a version of Alphabet Soup after her name. (Rabbit trail: Do kids still eat that stuff?) You see, many interpreters live in the fantasy that skill and certifications are the basis for being chosen for a job, but that mindset shows that, in some cases, and dare I say even perhaps most cases, in your average American towns, Deaf Consumers will often take a kind, easy going interpreter with a bit less skill over the Sign Language King/Queen who is crowned by his/her ego. Skill is important, but ego matters too.

One last issue to cover and you are home free. (You are ready to be done with this section, I know.) I am so proud that you have stuck it out with me. Some of you are saying, "Well, I don't think I have an ego." How do you self-assess your ego status? Let's take a completely unscientific ego-meter quiz.

THE COMPLETELY UNSCIENTIFIC YET QUITE "TELLING" EGO-METER QUIZ

1) Do you feel like it is worth your time to attend workshops in the areas you have the MOST experience?
   ❑ YES ❑ NO

2) Do you feel like you need mentoring?
   ❑ YES ❑ NO

3) Do you feel comfortable as an interpreter?
   ❑ YES ❑ NO

4) Does it bother you when someone suggests you change? ❑ YES ❑ NO

5) Are you excited to learn something new?
   ❑ YES ❑ NO

6) Do you often complain or argue?
   ❑ YES ❑ NO

7) Do you find yourself believing that the mistakes you make on the job are usually caused by your team interpreters, your inability to hear, the amount of prep time you were given, etc.? ❑ YES ❑ NO

8) Do you request or enjoy feedback?
   ❑ YES ❑ NO

9) Did this section make you uncomfortable?
   ❑ YES ❑ NO

10) Do you hate me right now?
   ❑ YES ❑ NO

SUGGESTED ANSWERS TO THE COMPLETELY UNSCIENTIFIC YET QUITE "TELLING" EGO-METER QUIZ

1) I might be known as a Performance Interpreter, but I still have much to learn in the field of interpreting, which includes the area of performance. I believe any individual striving to better him/herself even in areas where they feel the most comfortable, is making good and healthy non-ego choices. The ideal EF (Ego-Free) answer is "Yes".

2) EF terps always want to grow and are open to some form of mentoring at any stage of their careers. The ideal EF answer is "Yes".

3) I think EF interpreters never feel too comfortable. I have found that interpreters who battle ego tend to say, "I've got this." People all over the country look up to me as a Performance Interpreter, and even after literally thousands of musical interpretations, I still don't say to myself, "I've got this." I am still challenged in a unique way at every performance. I still make mistakes at every event. I think the ideal EF response is "No".

4) I believe EF terps relish in opportunities to change. None of us love to hear that we have "blown it" or "can improve" because we want to do our job perfectly. However a solid EF interpreter is ready to say, "Thanks for the

input." It doesn't mean the one offering the feedback is presenting suggestions which must be heeded, but the goal is being willing to listen to an opinion without offense. That's the key, listening without getting irritated, bothered, or offended. I think the ideal EF response is "No".

5) I think EF interpreters are always excited to learn something new. They want to grow and change. I found interpreters who don't feel they have much to learn on a particular subject, suffer from a bit of ego. A good EF response would be "No".

6) I have found, without question, interpreters who complain, blame, or argue a great deal have an ego problem. Many people misinterpret egotism as only being associated with arrogance, but arrogance is a kissing cousin to insecurity. A person with an ego is about the all-important "I". It encompasses both camps, the "I can" and the "I can't" interpreters. Interpreters with an ego want to shift the focus away from their own imperfection or lack, and they want to elevate their opinions and perspectives for the purpose of self-protection. How? The faithful three, complaining, blaming, and arguing. The ideal EF response is "No".

7) If your answer was "Yes", refer to number six.

8) EF terps see the benefit of consumer or team feedback. They see it as an opportunity to grow and change for the better. Again, not all feedback is beneficial or in keeping with your personal values or perspectives. That's ok. The ideal EF response is "Yes".

9) If you squirmed through this chapter, that could be a bad sign.

10) If you are ticked-off by what you have read, and are envisioning ways to either physically wound me, post nasty comments about me on your social networking pages, blast spite filled texts about me to your friends, or if you have left this chapter determined to never attend one of my workshops, I am guessing this hit closer to home than you would like to admit. If a weight has just been lifted off of your shoulders, you are ready to hug me, or you are conjuring up plans to build a monument in my honor, I am sure you have fallen victim to these egotistical behaviors. Let's say, the EF response here should be obvious.

The fact is that ego damages people's hearts, minds, souls, spirits, and interpretations. Ego negatively influences the environment and the relayed message. There is definitely a range of egotism as well. Some individuals are just a bit stubborn, overconfident, or insecure, yet have a manageable ego. Then there are *THOSE* interpreters who are the polar opposite, and they can be a greater challenge. In the end, egotistical interpreters are often the interpreters who inspire their teams and their consumers to buy a bazooka and risk jail time. These are some of the greatest hit man inspiring terps.

On a serious note, if you have just discovered ego was more a part of your life, or more damaging than you once realized, remember the words of Anne of Avonlea (from the "Anne of Green Gables" series), "Tomorrow is a new day, with no mistakes in it." You can always start fresh tomorrow.

FRUSTRATING INTERPRETER #2:
THE UNPROFESSIONAL INTERPRETER

Congrats! You survived the EGO section. We won't address it again so you are safe. Let's all take a deep breath. Even I admit, that was intense, but I believe it needed to be said. Ok, together... BREATHE IN... BREATHE OUT... BREATHE IN... BREATHE OUT... Let's picture butterflies, and little fairies, and Sam strung up by her ankles... OH NO! Not that! (Haha. Someone is saying, "Oh yes, *THAT!*") Let's picture flowers, and waterfalls, and little puppies... BREATHE... BREATHE... BREATHE... Ok, all cleansed.

Our next favorite hit man inspiring terp is *The Unprofessional Interpreter*. This could take days, and I assume you are not hoping to read a book the length of the entire Encyclopedia Britannica series so let me just hit some highlights. (Side note: for you youngin's, Encyclopedias used to be in book form not electronic form. We used to actually *go to the library* to read them rather than pull them up on Google or using an app on our phone. Crazy, huh?) Unprofessionalism can be reflected in attitude, ethical choices, attire, organizational skills, focus, preparation, interaction, and so on. Let's delve into a few of these, but reserve a few for later chapters. Topping our list of Unprofessional Interpreters is one with whom we often interact.

– The Lazy Interpreter –

Ah, yes, *The Lazy Interpreter*. They are the ones who don't want to prep prior to a job; they don't want to make an effort to serve while on a job, and they just don't care. We all have our lazy days when we are too tired to see straight or too sick to muster up the energy, etc. I am not talking about moments like those. I am talking about chronically lazy interpreters, interpreters who live under the mandate of "I just don't want to," "Can't you just do it?" "I just don't have the time," or a personal favorite, "Do I have to?" They hate doing anything uncomfortable, inconvenient, or uninteresting. Unprofessionalism manifested in laziness puts an undue burden on your team interpreter. It doesn't breed any friends either. So friends, grab those energy drinks, get excited to take on your interpreting assignments, and dig deep for enthusiasm and motivation. It's always a win/win situation.

– The Ranting Interpreter –

Outrageous *Ranting Interpreters* rank as number two among our interpreters with frustrating unprofessional behaviors. When on a job, interpreters need to leave their emotions at the door. It's tough, but personal problems can develop into some crusty emotional funk which can flake off during an assignment. Sometimes emotional outbursts include tears, anger, bitterness, or fear. Whatever the emotions, they need to be tabled when on the job.

I am not claiming perfection in this area. I had an incident where, on a particular day, a best friend had driven me to the edge. I went to a job, and I did the job. It was a normal collegiate interpreting assignment. My faux pas inched to the surface on break. The consumer and I had worked together for an extended period of time, and sadly she made the mistake of asking me how I was doing. Umm, not good. Have you seen **Monty Python and the Holy Grail**? One famous line would have been an homage to that day, "*RUN AWAY!*" She had a chance to make for the door, but she made the mistake of not only asking how I was, but waiting to hear my answer. Silly Deaf girl. Ladies, you know how men can make you crazy? This was one of those times. My BBF (Best Boy Friend) was in a "making Sam nuts" phase, and I had become pent up, a little too pent up. When asked, I blew-up in frustration like a block of TNT going off in a fireworks factory. Ok, that's an exaggeration; however, I did make my lack of happiness a little too apparent. This girl loved listening to people express their deep thoughts and emotions, so she was a good consumer with whom to vent, but was that professional? Not so much. It would have been more appropriate to chat about it when I was off site, or not at all, instead of discussing what was happening on break. In the end, no harm done. She laughed at outburst, even enjoyed the drama, and all was well. In all honesty, when I look back on that choice, I am disappointed in myself. I wouldn't accept that rant from myself today, and I wouldn't want my interpreters now to make a similar choice. Hindsight is 20/20.

Luckily that incident didn't have negative repercussions; however, I have seen unfettered emotions cause serious problems. There once was an interpreter named... (I can't say her name! That would be tacky.) Let's call her Betty. I went to teach a sign language class for Social Workers in Nashville. Knowing they were working with interpreters, I covered the responsibilities and roles of an interpreter while on assignment. I specifically targeted using interpreters in the mental health setting as that would be the venue for their use of interpreters. After a 15 minute lecture on working with an interpreter, one social worker said, "Are you saying interpreters are not supposed to talk about themselves on an assignment?" (Oh goody. Love where this is going.) "No, they are not." She tilted her head with a confounded look. "Really?" I knew whatever statements were to follow would, at minimum, throw me into a full blown asthma attack, far more critical than the immediately available inhaler in my purse could manage, at worse the story to come would send me into a full coronary. Nevertheless, I hoped for no medical issues, and did what was obviously physically risky but necessary; I asked her "Did that happen to you?" She replied, "Well... yes." (Oh please don't continue!) She continued, "I began talking with my client about sexual abuse and as soon as we got started the interpreter stopped us and told us her own story of sexual abuse. It took, like, 45 minutes, and in the end, the entire room was in tears. We couldn't emotionally recover from that in 15 minutes [when the appointment would end]. I felt bad for her, but I was a little frustrated we had lost our meeting time with the client." See, I told you it was bad.

If you are a professional interpreter you're probably thinking right about now, "Sam's hit man idea has some merit to it." Did you catch that? The interpreter stopped a counseling session to talk about herself, and her own, very personal, very emotionally charged, sexual abuse issues for 45 minutes! Then she left those present with a lap full of used Kleenexes and 15 minutes of meeting time to recuperate and cover their own topics! Are you kidding me? Her emotional rant radically impacted people's perspective of the field, and it clearly dismantled the appointment itself. Betty meant well, but she wasn't focused on doing her job, she was focused on herself.

– The Inattentive Interpreter –

Our third favorite unprofessional interpreter is *The Inattentive Interpreter*. Oh yeah, love them. These are the interpreters who feel availability is optional. I am not going to claim perfection on this one either. There are a few interpreting moments in my twenties and early thirties I look back on and think, "Re-do please." I have left for a bathroom break when a college student was focused on personal work for an extended period of time, and been stopped by someone in the hall and distracted longer than I should have been. No award there. However, let's talk about some more severe faux pas, shall we?

What are examples of substantial inattentive interpreter moments? Have you worked with a team who felt that her book or her phone was far more important than backing you up? Yeah, those people. Being inattentive for a moment isn't ideal, but the repeated inattentiveness of many interpreters is definitely damaging. I have heard some incredible inattentiveness stories. One day, I got called to an assignment for a Deaf individual with an extended stay in a local hospital. I arrived on site and the medical staff and I discussed how the situation should be handled, an interpreter's role, the needs of the particular patient, etc. The nurse said, "So you are going to be available the entire time you are here?" (NO, NOT AGAIN!) "Yes, I will. Did you have a problem with a previous interpreter?" (Please say "No," please say "No.") The nurse continued, "Well, she was assigned to the company's emergency pager. She was called in overnight, but when she got here she said that she had [medical condition deleted], and she was tired and needed to sleep. She decided she would sleep in an available room for the night, and told us if we needed to talk to the patient, we should just wake her. We didn't want to bother her though; so we just managed without her. We are so glad you are here and available for us. We are having a really hard time communicating with him." (Ya think?) Thank God that interpreter was not working for me because Sam was not happy. Am I missing something? The point of an emergency pager is that the interpreter is, I know this is big for some people, *available during an emergency!* Her body was there, but clearly she earned her badge as an *inattentive interpreter* that day.

This type of unprofessionalism is frustrating. It means services don't get rendered appropriately or effectively, and it means subsequent interpreters become responsible for managing and/or healing the wounds caused by the previous individual. Inattentive interpreters might have valid reasons for their mental interruption or disassociation, and that's understandable. There is no condemnation for that. We are human! If you are on an assignment when you find out your child has just been taken to a hospital, no one would ever blame you for your distraction, your frantic texts, or trips to the bathroom to sneak a phone call to see if your child is alive. There are literally thousands of valid scenarios for some form of inattentiveness. However intentionally ignoring your team because your latest romance novel has you entranced, because you are immersed in the latest Facebook posts, or because you just don't want to be physically present and it seems you can fashion a valid excuse for your absence, is not professional. These actions damage the assignment, the consumers, and forthcoming relationships. So, if that has poked at a few guilt spots, rethink some of those future choices and make your consumers and teams smile.

– The Late Interpreter –

Numero quatro: This interpreter is one of the favorites for the Deaf, *THE LATE INTERPRETER!* Disclaimer: We are not talking about that rare, "couldn't plan for it" or the "late one day" interpreter. I had a situation where I lived three or four suburban blocks away from an ongoing assignment. I could crawl to the assignment... in minutes, ...blindfolded, ...backwards. I never tried it mind you, but I could do it if I wanted. I left for work 20 minutes early for my 1 - 2 minute drive (3 with traffic). This particular situation needed the interpreter in the classroom 5 minutes prior to an assignment. I had plenty of time to spare, but I was 45 minutes late to the class that day. Why? A transformer blew out on the main road, and shut down every ounce of traffic. The street was a virtual parking lot. Since flames were shooting out of the tub on top of the electrical whatchamacallit, and the traffic was at a dead standstill, I knew I could be facing hours of waiting. I sat there for a while, but as class time fast approached, I opted for an alternative, which was not ideal, but what seemed my only option. I somehow slithered my way through the traffic, and weaved wildly in the opposite direction through various neighborhoods, ending up driving about 7 – 10 miles out of my way to get back to the street I needed to be on, so I could get to the job before the end of class. What a crazy experience! Maybe I should have abandoned my car and tried the crawling thing? Obviously, that was unpredictable and has never happened before or since. We are not discussing those random mishap type days. We are addressing chronic lateness.

One of the interpreters who works for me said the other day, "I have been going to a lot of jobs lately where I arrive 15 minutes early and the person on site says, 'You are already here?' I would ask them, 'Is this unusual?' and they would say 'Well, our interpreters normally arrive 15 – 20 minutes late. It's wonderful that you are here on time so we can get started.'" Oh, thank God that particular individual was not talking about interpreters from my agency. I don't want to do jail time for causing physical harm to my staff. Chronically late interpreters, especially interpreters arriving 15 and 20 minutes late to an assignment, are a problem. Clearly, that behavior is unprofessional, but it's also inconsiderate to all who are involved. I have actually known of a Deaf individual who dropped out of college, because one of the college's staff interpreters was often 15 – 30 minutes late. The loss of daily information threw the consumer so far behind that the student was unable to catch up in the course. That interpreter sabotaged that consumer's education. It's sad, and honestly, unacceptable.

– The Sleepy Interpreter –

Ok, our fifth prize winning unprofessional interpreter is *The Sleepy Interpreter.* Let me just own this one. I confess! I told you I was human, and this book is an homage to many of my own errors. This unprofessional label was one I wore all too often. In my twenties, I was working days as an interpreter, and nights as a lighting designer; I was a volunteer 10 – 20 hrs/week, and I fostered a teenager. Somewhere in that jumble of responsibilities I also had a hearty (yet innocent) social life. This left me with an average of two hours of sleep a night, which I bravely upped to four hours in my thirties and now that the years are catching up with me I am up to five or six in my forties. I would drag my sorry self through the work day. Sometimes I would literally be surviving the week solely through the infusion of caffeine. It wasn't ideal to say the least.

I have one story that, although I don't think it will win any professionalism awards, it was just flat out funny, and must be relayed in this section. I was an educational interpreter in my mid-twenties. I was given a math class because clearly my bosses hated me (in my mind that is the only reason any interpreter should be subjected to a math class). I cannot explain it, but every time I sit in a math class, I yawn. *EVERY TIME!* It could be at 10 o'clock in the morning, it could be at 3 o'clock in the afternoon, it doesn't matter; I yawn. One hour of sleep or twenty, it's irrelevant. I have a psychological condition. In fact, I just yawned when I started typing my story about interpreting a math class. I clearly have a problem! If you stop and couple that with an honest lack of sleep, you have a recipe for disaster. One day, I sat down in front of my two students to interpret their math class, one boy and one girl. It was math, so I yawned. That made the girl yawn, which made me yawn. That yawn was seen by the boy and it made him yawn, which made me yawn. That made both of them yawn, which made me yawn. A creative moment in this boy's thinking compelled him to grab a *MATH* book and stick it in front of his face as he yawned, which still made me yawn. (Note: It was a *MATH* book. Not helpful.) This then inspired the girl to put her head in her shirt so she could yawn, which still left me knowing she was yawning, which made me yawn. Then we all yawned openly together, and we finally all broke out into silent hysterics. (Did it just make you yawn?) No professionalism awards donated to me in honor of that incident, but you gotta admit, it's funny. At least it was funny to the three of us. (FYI: I no longer interpret math classes.)

Math mental health issues aside, in general, I arrived on assignments exhausted. I do have a slew of excuses, all of which are completely valid. I was working constantly. I had to in order to financially survive at the time. I was a parent. I was in my twenties and living as much as I could. I say it again, hindsight is 20/20. Looking back, I regret not being at my best every day. Did my exhaustion properly represent the Hearing or Deaf consumers? Did that appear professional to other individuals viewing the interpreter? No. I confess, it's one of the largest professionalism regrets I have in my career, and once I realized the implications of my exhaustion, I did my best to be on top of my game.

I have seen worse than just a tired interpreter though! I worked with a team terp who would fall asleep during class, and snore, *LOUDLY!* For me as a team interpreter, I found I often saw my 20 minute turn become 30 or 40 minutes because he wasn't awake to take over. He practically scared the bageebeez out of me every time he would snort and wake himself up, which he did often. His snoozing incidents occurred frequently, daily in fact. He embarrassed me beyond anything I can conjure into a written description. I felt like he was an embarrassment to the field, to our team, and most of all to the Deaf consumer. In the end, he never apologized, never attempted to make any personal changes, just assumed all individuals present should cater to his exhaustion.

Sleep improves language production and comprehension as well. When I haven't slept well for appropriate periods of time, I notice that I can lose focus when people are speaking or signing to me. I am not just referring to time on the job, but when I am really pooped, my brain doesn't process information rapidly or effectually in any venue or in any language. When I am really slammed with exhaustion, I can forget words like *cabinet* or *mailbox* in English, much less obliterate the beautiful picturesque nature of ASL as I sign. Comprehension of ASL on a truly bad day? When I am incredibly sleep deprived and my focus is shot, it takes me four or five seconds to realize someone has lifted their hand to fingerspell, much less me grasp their finger flapping and convert that into a readable word. In the end, sleep deprivation creates limitations, and if I plan to communicate in any language, teach or interpret, I have to sleep some, or there is no hope of success. No more all-nighters. No more trying to finish a project rapidly before the sun comes up (well I still do that on occasion, but not when I have to interpret the next day). If I am going to be effective at my job, I need to sleep. (And all my students, friends, and co-workers say, "AMEN!")

So people... get some sleep! Find a way! I know sometimes you are just stuck. Single moms nursing all night are not going to show up perky to a job the next day unless they have truly mastered the art of managing interrupted sleep. If you have to work multiple jobs to survive, tiredness is understandable; however, dragging on the job because you are partying all night long, because you are catching up on the latest soap operas late at night, because you are just a night owl (my temptation) and won't to go to bed, or because you refuse to visit a sleep specialist for medical intervention with your personal sleep disorder, can be avoided. Sleep my friends! I will too, and all of our clients will have great happiness and joy.

– The Slouchy Interpreter –

The Slouchy Interpreter: These are the people, often hunched over, poorly dressed, uninterested; they are individuals who don't present themselves in an appropriate professional manner. You see them in schools, religious institutions, and freelancing. They are everywhere. Most of us have been a slouchy interpreter one day or another, and for many of you it's a daily lifestyle which could stand a little reevaluation. Since I am clearly risking all respect by confessing my many interpreting sins, let's add another to the mix. Sam story number, who knows what, here it goes: I was having a particularly bad day when I was 23 and working in schools. I was interpreting for a smart aleck teen who had an IQ far above my own. I remember him as being smart, funny, and incredibly sarcastic. That boy was undoubtedly one of the highlights of my interpreting career. I adored working with him, however interpreting for him was a roller coaster ride. At one point of the semester I wasn't doing well. I had faced a rough night, rough day, at that point, a rough life, and I just didn't care about much of anything. One day, I went to work and did my job, but as the day went on, I went downhill. My hair hadn't been "done" that day (not that anyone can do much with my Greek/Lebanese "fro" on any day), my makeup was minimal, and I looked pretty rough. At one point my lack of enthusiasm was a little too apparent, as I ended up sliding so far into my chair, I was nearly seated horizontally. Then, revelation struck. I suddenly stopped and looked at myself to my own horror. I stepped out of my role briefly and said "I must not be a pretty site to look at right now, am I?" He sat there, eyebrow twisted up, brimming with his sarcastic wit, and jerked his head to the side rapidly and said, "Nope." I immediately sat up straight, dug deep for some energy and enthusiasm and started interpreting with all the oomph I could muster. I felt the tone, the accuracy, and the effectiveness of the message change as my presentation changed. I never behaved like that on an assignment again.

That moment in my early career wasn't a professional one. I told you I wasn't perfect. I wish I could say I was the only one who has ever made those personal errors, but I frequently see interpreters present themselves as slouchy, uninterested, barely mobile, and unkempt, and I feel bad for the Deaf. Why should they have to suffer because of our issues? It's not right. That was a day that I started to see things through Deaf eyes, and so, although I can't say that moment of my youth was one of which I am proud, it did make an impact on everything I do today. So people, stop, look at yourself, and think of what your consumers see and prefer, then make a few changes accordingly.

– The Excuse Driven Interpreter –

Alright, the Chronically Late Interpreter definitely inspires a hit man, the Slouchy Interpreter probably only inspires a trip to Home Depot for the purchase of a 2x4, however *The Excuse Driven Interpreter* should reignite the passion for at least a minimal ammo purchase. "I just couldn't because...," "She didn't do it because...," "We didn't know ahead of time so...," "If only I could have had... then I could....," "I can't hear. I can't hear. I can't hear. I can't hear." Goodness! I have traveled the country and asked the Deaf what aspect of interpreters frustrated them the most, and the primary repeated complaint was "excuses from an interpreter". I was shocked! I had never pictured that bothering the Deaf like it did. What are commonly used excuses? The Deaf will hear about why interpreters weren't prepared, why they couldn't hear, why they couldn't do their job, why they couldn't be at a job on time, why they couldn't stand in the proper place, why they couldn't advocate for better Deaf seating, why they struggle working with their team, etc. After the shock of this onslaught of similar complaints settled into my exhaustion ridden brain, I stepped into the shoes of the Deaf and considered what I have seen over the years. Upon reflection, I have to say, I get it. That would drive me bonkers too!

Think about it. It makes complete sense. The Deaf want you to arrive on site, do your job, and go home. Most don't want a dissertation on our problems as an interpreter, or challenges with the particular job we have been called to do. Yet we feel compelled to give them an explanation. Yes, it's true, sometimes there needs to be an explanation of a conflict or challenge, but that explanation should be brief, professional, mature, and not excuse driven. It should be presented as a quick statement of fact, and the problem then managed accordingly. Overblown excuses truly are rampant in our field. I have seen many. The truth is, these excuse driven remarks are usually founded in our insecurities, and those insecurities wreak havoc in many ways. (Oh no, more wreaking!) Clearly, our consumers want us to strive for professionalism and leave our excuses behind.

Readers! Fellow Terps! Please state that you can't hear once and then sign what you can. Your team didn't prepare? Do your best, since you did. Positioning is bad? If they complain, briefly explain your advocacy and then interpret. Keep explanations to an as needed basis and keep them brief, positive, and professional. Avoid any immature blaming. I know we all want to explain the problems at hand (and let's be honest, we don't want to look bad in front of our consumers), but too much is unprofessional. Remember again, keep explanations: brief, positive, and professional. Your consumers will thank you.

– The Scene Making Interpreter –

The next jail time inspiring unprofessional terp is *The Scene Making Interpreter.* These are the interpreters who bring drama with them wherever they go. Sometimes the interpreter presents himself/herself as completely normal prior to the boisterous unavoidable expression of unfettered drama, but often these terps walk into a room and the drama enters just prior to their arrival, then parts people like Moses and the Red Sea. These interpreters are the ones who inspire more than a bazooka rental, but rather the presence of an entire regimen of bazooka carrying militia. Sometimes they show up on a job ready to start spouting the tenets of the ADA (Americans with Disabilities Act) to anyone they deem possibly threatening or denigrating to their consumers. Other times they show up on a job demanding equipment at the last minute assuming concert crews are available to meet their needs at whim. Sometimes they show up on a job with loud voices piercing anyone's hearing within earshot causing quite a stir. Still other times, they show up on job waving an agenda, thought to be untouchable, and become irate when plans change, as they inevitably do. No matter what happens, they always show up on a job focused almost entirely on themselves and usually with some form of complaint in hand, ready to be propelled at any individual who inadvertently walks across his/her path.

When we stop and consider the CPC (Code of Professional Conduct) its theme breeds equality and anonymity. The truth is, these interpreters might sometimes think their endgame is to create equality, but usually their methods of getting to this elusive equality lend themselves to more division and negativity than was ever necessary. It is also obvious that anonymity is never on the agenda of a Scene Making Interpreter... never. They want their voices heard and often at the expense of everything and everyone in their immediate vicinity.

I was on a performance job once where my team interpreter's arrival preceded my own by a few minutes. She walked in and began an audacious declaration of her needs, which she clearly saw as being primary, and it was apparent she felt those needs should be immediately fulfilled by all crew members. I was horrified by her behavior. Having spent my life on various crews in concert and theatrical settings, I knew the work those individuals were facing over the next hour, and I knew her needs, compared to the thousand things which would in fact stop their show entirely if not accomplished, were miniscule in their minds. She did herself, and honestly, the field, a tremendous disservice by attempting to create a scene to get what she wanted. Those crew members would remember interpreters as pushy and unreasonable after that incident, and that saddened me.

Now, some interpreters who should attend OTA (Overdramatic Terps Anonymous) are not making demands, they have an entirely different set of behaviors to propel at the oncoming victims of their drama. For example: I was on another performance job and one of the people in charge walked up to me and said, "You are one of the interpreters?" (Another one? Can I just say, "No?") "Yes," I responded, hoping I could crawl under the stadium seating as he glanced around the venue. He said, "Well, your companion has been backstage bothering the artists. Please get rid of her. We don't want to work with her again." Yippee! Another gem. Once again, what was the impression left by that interpreter? By the time she left, they saw all interpreters as over-ambitious and obsessive. Our job is never supposed to negatively influence an environment. In this case, the interpreter was a fan, and under the guise of "advocacy" she was getting her one-on-one time with the artists (singers) she loved.

These Scene Making Interpreters sometimes walk onto a job spouting commands, or sometimes criticisms, sometimes, clearly they are fans or advocates for a particular cause, but all of these interpreters are a problem. As for advocacy, we cannot walk onto a job like a bulldozer, we need a softer touch. Yes, advocacy is important, and sometimes advocacy needs less honey and more vinegar, but so often advocacy is an excuse for what I call "Interpreter Bullying," the unsuspected attack from interpreters under the guise of advocacy. That's never acceptable. Interpreters need boundaries and the drama needs to be left at the door.

– The Unethical Interpreter –

Our final tempting target is *The Unethical Interpreter*. Right now I know you are likely able to relay 20 of your own stories. The Code of Professional Conduct is, in fact, a wonderful creation, and I commend the writers of this document. The way to define our role as an interpreter is complicated, but these creators have done it successfully. They have given us a good vision of efficacious interpreting and I clap boldly for their efforts. Ethics are a critical part of being a professional interpreter, so clearly logic of course, dictates that an interpreter not following our basic Code of Professional Conduct would of course be defined as an *Unprofessional Interpreter*.

Who else can fall in this section? There are so many examples, I could write a book reminiscent of War & Peace if I wanted to list them all, but you would hate me, and likely not buy my next book, so let's stop here. You have a number of concepts to ponder, so ponder away and let's move onto number three.

FRUSTRATING INTERPRETER #3:
THE UNSKILLED INTERPRETER

We have all been there. We have been our imperfect selves on a job, in over our heads, floundering, begging God for help, unless you don't believe in God (however there is nothing like an assignment heading straight for disaster to get ya to consider that there might in fact be a God). Hopefully, that has happened only rarely in our careers, but for most of us it *HAS* happened. My ITP wasn't perfect, but they did a great job emphasizing that we should never take a job until we were qualified. I have worked hard to try and maintain that perspective.

I have moved from my amazing home in Southern California and presently reside in Tennessee. Tennessee is beautiful! It's so green! I honestly feel like it could possibly be the most beautiful state in the Union (although I know many of you feel the same about your homes) and of course living in Music City has its perks. We live among the biggest names in the industry. We eat with people you listen to on the radio. We shop with people you see on stage. Johnny Depp just moved to town and now has a house near our office. Let's hope he wants to take sign language classes. This town is bizarre, but it's so much fun. If you love music, there's no better place to be. So, unmistakably, this town has characteristics you will adore, but we also have a few issues. One undeniable problem is that we have absolutely no requirements for interpreters. I have heard a rumor that EIPA (Educational Interpreter Performance Assessment) certification is required for educational interpreters, but at the time of writing this book, I have yet to see it enforced in Middle Tennessee. I know ASL II students placed in full time educational interpreter positions. I know interpreters earning a decent salary who learned sign language from a book, only one book, maybe only half of one book, in fact. Trusting the skills of interpreters in this town, can be tricky.

One day, I had a girl come into the office. She was considering getting evaluated to become one of our interpreters, or possibly to become one of our Sign language students (Note: She requested entering our "sign language" *NOT* "interpreting" program.) Anyone raise an eyebrow at that statement? I did. I had a bad feeling about her before she even stepped in the door, and after meeting her, my concerns were quickly justified. When she sat down it took about two nanoseconds to conclude she had no idea what it meant to be an interpreter. She then informed me she had been working in schools. I told her I needed to evaluate her skills before I could recommend either classes or a position as an interpreter. I knew a full evaluation wasn't necessary, so I kept it simple. I started to talk a little about ASL grammar. After a statement about ASL syntax, something commonplace as adjectives appearing after nouns, she professed with incredible enthusiasm, "We learned that in school!" My bad feeling was getting worse. Needless to say, she couldn't sign a single sentence in ASL. She had a good heart, but I undoubtedly had concern about her serving as a language example in schools.

Honestly, I don't think the fault lies completely with the interpreters; the schools should be more aggressive about pursuing qualified personnel. One day we will have better laws in place. Ironically, although Tennessee has some scary interpreter personnel in place, we also have some of the absolute best interpreters in the country. Life is interesting here. Since we can't fix Tennessee's laws today, let's keep talking about Scary Interpreter #3, *The Unskilled Interpreter,* those people with whom you land on assignment, and who can really inspire a "Buy a hit man" loan.

As interpreters we need to accept a job equivalent to our skill level, or possibly just slightly above, so we are constantly challenging ourselves to grow. Interpreters who arrive on a job and lack the vocabulary and grammar needed to accurately present the information, do a disservice to the Deaf and the Hearing. I have had interpreters say, "Well, I need the practice." That sounds valid, but there are assignments and mentoring relationships where practice is appropriate and manageable, and there are many assignments where it is far less than ideal. When an interpreter accepts an assignment far beyond his/her skill level, the result of that decision can be quite detrimental to both the Deaf and the Hearing Consumers.

We were working with an actor from L.A. His friends are the faces of Deaf names you see on the small and big screen. He told us about a time when a group of Deaf actors gathered to attend what, in retrospect, I remember as being a Hollywood awards show. Don't quote me on it. As the event went on, the Hearing crowd laughed, the Deaf did not. The crowd was engrossed in speeches from fellow actors, the Deaf were not. Hour by hour there was an obvious discrepancy between what the Deaf and the Hearing were experiencing, and from what I heard, it became unbearable. After the close of the event, the Deaf consumers complained about the interpreter, and were told it was a student, or students who wanted to practice their skills and were hired based on their willingness to volunteer. They wanted to volunteer in this type of venue? The Deaf deserved better. If the communication is unclear, inaccurate, choppy, or even immature, it can become utterly frustrating to view as the consumer, plus it might encourage the consumer to pay off a hit man.

We have looked at a lot of issues regarding interpreter conduct in this chapter. This chapter of course made a lot of people uncomfortable. No one wants to know they have made an error. The greater question here is "Who is our priority?" Are our consumers, both Deaf and Hearing, our primary concern? Are our team Interpreters on our list of consideration? If not, are the thoughts in the forefront of our minds those of our own comfort, opinions, feelings, emotions, wants and needs? I believe we have to put ourselves aside, and in the end we should strive to be the kind of interpreter that doesn't inspire a hit man.

TERZIS' TIPS

$$E=MC^2$$

DON'T BEND THE RULES

What's the big deal if you bend the rules... just a little? Don't let this mindset sneak into your head. I *HAVE*, and I have paid for it. Here's an example. Standard rule: "Never interpret and chew gum." One day, I got up to interpret at a church service. I threw a piece of gum into my mouth as my throat was dry. My intention was not to chew on it, but rather just to suck on the rule breaking chewable substance while on duty. It sounded innocent enough. Ah, yes, the stories of my ongoing imperfection continue. 15 minutes or so into the service, I suddenly had to sneeze. I am not one of those people who will barely sneeze and follow it with a cute squirrely "Achoo." I sneeze with a vengeance. My body believes in expelling any and all things which might be causing the problematic tickle; and so it began. The sneeze started building, and building, and building, and then it happened; it hit so hard, and so fast, all I could do was cover my mouth and wail. Not pretty. My hand was covered in nastiness, and perched happily amid the grotesque expulsion was my wad of gum. Now, I was in front of 500 people, and everyone heard the mammoth blow, so eyes were on me, I had no doubt. What do I do? I mean, hey, there were two major problems at hand (oh, bad pun). One, my hand was gooey, and two, there was a wad of gum in it, so no subtle hand swipe against the back of my leg was going to solve my prevailing dilemma. Uh oh. The look on my face must have indicated what was happening because I saw giggles start to surface around the Deaf section. They knew. I was busted, and no one moved one inch to help me. Bad church people! They were having way too much fun to intervene. So, I decided to interpret... with one hand. I went on and on and on, and eventually they realized they weren't going to get as effective of a message with a single handed interpretation. Finally, someone, in an act of mocking-based assistance, subtlety walked up and placed a Kleenex on the stairs next to me, thereby empowering me to remedy my ghastly predicament, and mildly redeem my rule bending faux pas, at least to a point.

What's the moral of the story? Well, I guess on one level, learn to sneeze with less vigor, but globally, don't bend the rules. They are there for a reason, and although you might get away with skirting the standards one day, you might just pay for it the next. Clearly, *I DID!*

What **NOT** to Wear

We all have moments in our career which we regret. As you notice, I have had plenty. A number of them, I confess, are attire related. I can't say that as a twenty-something year old I made the best decisions in building a proper interpreter wardrobe, but that motivates me even more to teach others to make choices their consumers will love. Girls, clearly your garment choices relate to me more than those of our male counterparts, so I am targeting you all a bit more. Guys, have no fear, you can't escape this chapter! You all might think dressing for your interpreting assignments is simple, but every day in America the rules are broken. Let's take a look.

— UNDERwear —

Girls, this is more of an issue that you may think. It probably took me over 10 years to realize I had "an **under**wear problem," and as I note the error of my ways here, I hope you all can get inspired to do as I say, not as I did. If you are a newbie, I hope you choose to skip my decade of Deaf torture. If you are more seasoned, and you too have slipped up in this area in years gone by, I hope you will end all Deaf persecution and plan a future filled with appropriate *under*garments. Guys, stick with me. We will get to you, but first I need to have a heart-to-heart with the ladies.

The Over the Shoulder Boulder Holder

I have had all kinds of bra based incidents as an interpreter, some funny, some embarrassing, but one truth has become refined in my thinking, *BRAS MATTER!* You might say "It's just a bra!" That bra can impact an interpreter's day in so many ways. Picking the right one is critical!

Wearing a Bra

Some interpreters are a bit more "earthy" than others. Some feel bras are optional. You might be one of those people. I have complete respect for a wide variety of off job clothing perspectives, but on the job, I believe bras are vital to a less distracting wardrobe. You might think, "What does it matter?" Interestingly enough, I have questioned Deaf individuals from all over the country and one thing is for certain, many of them have strong opinions about the importance of the right bra! Who would have thought? I have nearly flown into hysterics as I teach the "Attire" section of my workshop and emphasize the use of appropriate and effective undergarments. I have seen Deaf heads nod in agreement with such stamina they look like bobblehead dolls on the dashboards of construction

74

trucks blasting over mud moguls. So the nods have led to questions, and the questions have led to answers, and the answers have led to stories, and the fact becomes quite apparent, bras *MATTER*! Or more accurately, the *RIGHT* bra matters.

I have searched the internet looking at hundreds of pictures of interpreters at events from conference interpreting to concert interpreting and it's clear, a woman's chest can be completely inconspicuous or incredibly distracting. I am attracted to men not women (Orlando Bloom and Shemar Moore rank quite high on the Sam list of males over which to ogle. Silly me. I digress.) Even from the perspective of a straight woman, an undergarment-free woman, on a stage, interpreting with great movement, draws my attention, as it does with much of the audience. This might be effective for winning a date, but most of the audience will not be focusing on the movement of her *HANDS*. The interpretation will suffer. The fact is that, as interpreters we strive to *blend*, and wearing a bra becomes a critical part of the blending process. Without one, you can quickly become the source of much attention and conversation, and *not positive* attention and conversation, mind you. The structure of our chests means things poke out or hang in ways which draw the wandering eye when not properly secured. So secure the girls and let's refrain from undue visual distractions.

What about tank tops? I have seen interpreters feel that braless tanks are a sufficient remedy for their hatred of bras. The problem is that the lack of support, leads to less controlled chest movement and body parts poking through thin material. That lends itself to potential visual disruption. For those of us "blessed" but not "too blessed" (a D or under), a tank, if it has a solid built in bra, usually can work when worn under something with more coverage on the shoulders and when the tank doesn't allow for visual protrusions. So earthy folks, think tanks with significant secondary control and you are set! Those of you with a mighty blessing up above, probably need to consider the ol' fashioned bra for your most effective support. Tanks won't quite serve as "blessing control" when on the job.

A general question to serve as a guideline when picking your attire, both under and over is, "What will my consumers think?" Many interpreters wear (or don't wear) clothes based on their personal preferences, but what they don't realize that *their* preferences are often not the preferences of their consumers. Before you ban a bra, stop and think what your consumers prefer. You might like to feel free, but after having heard complaints from coast to coast about bras, or the lack thereof, I can definitively tell you that consumers may feel more strongly about your choices than you realize.

The RIGHT Over the Shoulder Boulder Holder

The *RIGHT* bra is an important part of every interpreter's wardrobe. One day, I realized how often I had bra problems. *The Double Divas* on TLC have a point. We should invest in our chests. (Please note: I saw that on a commercial when flipping channels, I personally don't watch that show.) The fact is my slanted shoulders, and my habitual unwillingness to try on clothes before I buy them, often allows for a boulder holder quandary. I have purchased bras with straps which wouldn't stay up, some with band too tight, and others featuring underwires which wouldn't remain in in place. (Is this TMI? Haha.) The fact is that I had to adjust them regularly to get comfortable. In the end, I started thinking about how frustrating it would be to watch me yank at a strap, pull a band, or twist an underwire over and over again. I realized that my brassiere problem was not just my own, but one to which my consumers were subjected. Ouch!

I have funny stories to tell, mind you. For example: one day I was interpreting at a church and my underwire broke through the material and kept creeping up the center of my chest. (Girls, many of you know what I am talking about.) I would interpret until my consumer blinked or looked away, then I would quickly and discreetly shove it down with my thumb. It would creep up again, he would glance at the stage, and I would shove it down. This ritual continued the entire service. What an enjoyable day. One time, years later, in a college class the same thing happened, but that underwire was sharp and poked into my flesh with a vengeance. Pain and minor blood loss meant more radical intervention was required. When my consumer looked away, I grabbed that sucker and ripped it straight out of my bra and hid it under my leg. Ha! Neither that consumer, nor any student in the room, ever knew what had happened. I have to admit, it was a pretty smooth move. Yeah, I know someone is saying, "Why didn't you just excuse yourself and go to the bathroom?" It was a long class, I was the only interpreter on a high paced assignment, and there was no break coming. Don't judge! It had to be done, but at least I did it with speed and flair. Another time, I had a bra break on assignment. That one required a restroom trip and a slight changing of my arm positions for the remainder of the class to keep the girls where they belong. Goodness, then there are those straps I fought. It took me years to figure out I could tighten those enough to keep them on. So, now I purchase bras that hold the girls at precisely the perfect height, with the perfect straps, with underwires that stay in place. Lo and behold, I don't mess with my bra much at all. I bet there are all kinds of Deaf individuals out there that wish I had figured this out in my twenties.

Why the speech about bras? The fact is that anything you do to adjust your clothing breaks the flow of your message. It sometimes leads to a break in eye contact. It can get you out of character. It can just flat out be a distraction, or in some cases, the beginning of alluring thoughts for your consumers. The goal of every interpreter is to never draw attention away from the message, and clothing adjustments do just that.

What about nursing moms? I don't need to mention the importance of wearing multi-layer pads in your bras. All your consumer needs is for you to be interpreting when a baby cries, then suddenly the front of you looks like you walked chest first into a waterfall. Ladies with babies, buy thick bras, then purchase and use multiple bra pads so "oopses" don't happen.

Thin bra wearers, you all are not excluded from this conversation! You might feel like your thin bra is fabulously comfortable, but if your headlights turn bright when it is cold, or hot, or for whatever reason, you need to reevaluate. If you are at risk of an unwanted "howdy" from your upper half, buy padded bras! I know they are thicker and hotter but in the end you do not need any protrusions when interpreting. It's tacky and distracting.

I think that covers it. Girls! Grab your bank card and go buy a great bra, or two, or three, and make a commitment to keep your presentation focused on the message rather than the packaging you have been given. Don't lie to yourself about the relevance of our trusty *under*wear. Whether they tell you or not, your consumers will appreciate the effort!

Undies

This is brief (no pun intended). Girls, if they creep, or lie permanently embedded in private locations, leave them at home. Buy undies you don't need to pick at, pull at, twist, adjust, etc. Deaf people just love when their interpreters have ongoing wedgies.

Opt for Hanes over Thongs and going commando is risky, (and from my personal standpoint, kinda gross), so be careful and choose an underwear option which is safe and requires no intervention while on the job.

MMS

It seems appropriate in the undergarment section to cover MMS (Mid-Menstrual Syndrome). When Aunt Flo is here for a visit, girls, please make sure you have appropriately guarded yourself to make sure that there is no visual presentation of outward flowing fluids.

(Men! You love this section, don't you?

Hang in there. I will get to you).

Many of us can admit that at times we have interpreted and then done the "stand up and look" routine just to make sure nothing penetrated our protective measures. I have seen some girls, especially young interpreters, forget that a long assignment sometimes doesn't allow for bathroom stops, and that means extra protection, *BEFORE* you leave the house. So ladies, be wise and make sure protection is in place and able to serve.

Men! It's your turn!

Here's the deal. Tighty-whities are not supposed to be so tight that you need to readjust constantly. Buy the right size underwear. Guys, I know you all say adjustment is just a part of manhood, and I don't pretend to have any understanding of that particular packaging, but please consider two things: first, people rarely find that attractive so let's just call it an outright distraction from your message, and second, no matter how subtle you think you are being when moving your manhood around, WE NOTICE, so work towards making it as little of a necessity as possible. Again, your job is to present the message and although your comfort is ideal, the message can be skewed or harassed by the boys being diverted from location to location while interpreting. (And all the women say, "AMEN!")

— OUTERwear —

A trip through YouTube can send an instructor like me to the "funny farm". I can't believe the things interpreters in America wear! Bright pink shirts, bright red shirts, t-shirts bought at Wal-Mart 10 years ago, which have clearly been washed at least 224 times, non-opposing colors, severely wrinkled clothing, Hawaiian prints (and that one nearly drove me to drink), clothes Goodwill would reject without a thought, shirts with enormous brand names printed across them, or a personal favorite, a bright electric teal/blue suit with a huge swaying feathered broach or applique (which honestly looked like it could possibly be alive) perched at the shoulder. (That one would have to be Sam's second inspiration for alcohol consumption). It's horrendous! I hate that I need to add this section to the book, but I think there is no doubt that this needs to be addressed. Presentation matters! European interpreters might be more flexible with this, but as professionals in America, we need to maintain the standard of the field here. So let's start with color, shall we?

Colorama

It's standard American interpreting practice to wear colors opposing our skin tones. That means if you are dark, you wear light colors and vice versa. Let me emphasize, if you are dark skinned, "classic black" is NOT for you! Don't do it! I know a handful of ITPs out there have said, "All interpreters wear black," but that is an incredible misnomer! The goal is for your hands and arms to be easily seen. If you have dark skin, and you put on a dark outfit, then you stand in shadows, you are toast. There is little to no hope of being seen with ease. In that situation, eye strain is one problem. The interpreter completely disappearing and the consumer getting NO interpretation is a real possibility and a slightly bigger issue. So, dark skinned terps, wear your soft pastels; choose light blues, light lavenders, light greens, and yes, you can wear white. Just make sure your colors are opposing your skin tone.

Light skinned terps: most of you have heard this throughout your ITPs. Wear dark colors. Wear jewel tones. You should be in dark burgundy, dark green, dark blue, dark purple, and yes, of course, black. Some interpreters are thinking "We know this." If everyone knew and abided by the basic guidelines of interpreter attire, I wouldn't face oxygen deprivation from a trip around YouTube, much less a potential coronary when I walk past conference interpreters in their "acceptable interpreter attire". Even my own interpreters, who hear me preach this stuff time and time again, sometimes show up at my office with outfits that make me cringe! It seems very "Interpreter 101" yet here we are, 50 years into this field, and still professional working interpreters make a vast array of bad color choices every single day. The best part, the entire time, these interpreters believe in and defend their clothing choices.

Color No-No's

A color no one should ever, ever, ever, ever, ever, (please note my emphasis here), *EVER* wear is **RED**. Red is bad. It's hard on the eyes. You can try and justify that it's a "dark color," but unless it is dark brick red or burgundy it is still just **RED,** and it's a foul color choice. Let me take a moment to target dark skinned terps:

- o <u>Strong Pinks and Corals:</u> those are also hard on the eyes. If you are dark skinned and thought, "But no one has ever complained about it," just remember the goal is to make watching you as easy as possible. "No complaints" does not necessarily equal "personal preferences". Those colors could work if they are soft, but strong versions of those colors are always a problem.

- o <u>Oranges and Yellows:</u> Don't make me even say it. Those are a resounding "NO!"

- o <u>Tans and Browns:</u> I know some of you are about to lose half your wardrobe with this suggestion, but no skin tone opposes tans or browns. They can create eye strain. They are not the worst color, but they still are not ideal.

I know. Some of you have already texted your friends and asked, "Do you mind if I wear...?" Usually the answer back will be, "No, it's fine," because Deaf people are very tolerant on the whole. However, the goal is not for your previous choices to be justified, but instead to make our consumers' experiences as pleasant and easy as possible. Life as a Deaf person is challenging enough without the added strain of interpreter wardrobe conflicts.

Now for light skinned terps: is there a problem with bright versions of jewel tones? There can be.

- o <u>Royal Blue:</u> This is fine if it is not piercing-obnoxious-mind-numbing royal blue.
- o <u>Strong Greens:</u> These are generally fine, but if they look like Kermit in an erupting nuclear power plant you might want to step away. A jewel tone which is so bright it will knock your socks off defeats the whole concept of an easy background to visually manage.

What colors are ideal? For dark skinned terps, cool pastels are fabulous, colors like light blues, light lavenders, light greens, light teals, etc. White can be acceptable if the color and lighting doesn't make you look like the surface of the sun, however white can in some cases also be quite hard on the eyes. For light skinned terps, cool deep jewel tones like dark burgundy, dark blue, dark green, dark violet, dark teal and of course the infamous blacks are all acceptable. All of these will cause the least amount of eye strain, especially when under stage or TV lights. Remember, your goal is to best serve your clients. At least we are not stuck wearing scrubs every day!

I often hear arguments from dark skinned interpreters like, "I am not *THAT* dark. Can't I wear black?" True, there are some people who are neither light skinned nor dark skinned. They fall into that mystifying medium skinned category. Some of these individuals do well with almost any color, or need dark colors in the winter and light colors in the summer. If that is you, just remember, the goal is to create a clear and easy background for your signs. It's important to pick colors that will do just that. How do you assess? Experiment. Grab a dark and light shirt, go into a poorly lit room with a mirror, and place your arms in front of both color shirts to evaluate which color contrasts more, allowing your arms and skin to be seen with greater ease. Why a poorly lit room? Many interpreters don't realize how much room lighting effects how skin can be seen. Many dark skinned interpreters say, "Black is fine. You can still see my hands." Recently, we saw a black interpreter on TV who chose to wear black daily. She was never easy to see as she chose not to wear contrasting colors, but when she stood in dark areas of the studio, seeing her signs clearly was nearly impossible. There is power in evaluating your attire in a poorly lit room. Often interpreters don't have the luxury of great lighting, so if your skin color hits a middle ground, take a few moments one day to do some personal assessment.

Are colors on your lower half important? YES! Light skinned interpreters make the mistake every day of wearing darks on top and lights or printed materials on bottom. Stop right now, and do this little exercise with me. Stand up. Let your arms hang to your sides. Go ahead, do it. Don't just sit there reading this book. I have a point to make, and a visual aid will bring it home, so work with me. Stand up. Place your hands at your sides. Where do they land? On your thighs. Many words in ASL/Contact pass in front of our thighs which means it *IS* important to follow the same rules on your lower half as you do on your upper half.

One Piece, Two Piece, Three Piece

Suits pose the biggest problem. Let's first talk to men with darker skin. Suits only come in limited colors these days, unless you want to look like a disco dancer from the 1970's (please don't). If you have dark skin, the readily available black suit isn't my pick for you (obviously). I would opt for a light gray or light tan suit. Neither color is my preference, as neutral colors do not display enough opposition to skin tones. They don't create a clear and easy background; however if you are required to wear a suit, and you do have very dark skin, it's one of the only remaining options.

Light skinned men, oh my goodness, I need a moment. (Taking a moment.) Wait, I need two moments. Many of you have been stressing-out Sam for years. I am about to say all this in love, boys. Let's stop to analyze a commonly chosen ensemble, or two, or what the heck, let's analyze three. A black suit jacket with a light blue shirt and black tie does not constitute an appropriate solid dark background. That is a multicolored, multi-toned background. A medium-light gray suit with a lavender shirt and a lavender printed tie does not constitute a dark background. That is a light ensemble *WITH A PATTERN!* (Oh, help me... not a pattern again!) A black suit with a red shirt and a black and red tie, well... (I need another moment), please, don't make me explain why *THAT* doesn't constitute a solid dark background. (When I saw that one recently, I nearly had to call 911) I can't resist, I need a fourth example: a pin *STRIPED* suit *NEVER* constitutes a solid dark background. It has stripes! Gentlemen, friends, co-workers, interpreting family, I know the mindset is, "Well, my jacket it dark, so what does it matter?" The first problem with this philosophy is that your hands don't just remain over the left or right side of your chest while interpreting (at least I hope they don't), they move all over your thoracic region. Additionally, the secondary lighter or bright color draws attention, especially when the second color chosen is (I need a final moment...) RED! The same color rules apply to you. If you have to wear a suit, a black jacket with a black shirt and a black tie are not only considered sexy in the minds of most people, but it makes a very effective background for your signs (call it a "win-win"). If you want color, try a black jacket with a dark eggplant (purple) shirt and a solid dark eggplant tie. That can work. Please guys, save the red and the light green for your romantic evenings out. Dark skinned guys, apply the same rules previously discussed, just use opposite colors. I know for a few of you, again, I have disfigured your wardrobe. That isn't my intention. My only goal is to serve your consumers well.

While I am on a suit soap box, let's talk about those complicated ensembles a bit more in depth. I am not a huge proponent of suit jackets and/or ties. Jackets are restrictive, and ties flop around. I had one interpreter argue with me stating that he would wear them with a tie clip. Well, any aggressive male interpreter knows a tie clip can be a hazard as signs can land themselves under a tie allowing for the semi-secured tie and clip to be forcibly and disastrously removed in mid-sentence. Even a simple jerk can cause a shirt to get discombobulated. (I needed an excuse to use that word, and now, I have one.) Another interpreter told me he would wear ties with a sweater vest. Have you noticed ties can work their way out of a sweater vest? I have seen it, and the poor interpreters wearing them spend a significant amount of time jerking at their ties and breaking the flow of their message. Recently, I did see an interpreter wear a high vest with a tie significantly secured under the vest. He could easily interpret. It looked doubtful that the tie could work its way out. I think it was the first time I approved of how a tie was worn. In the end, whenever possible, I prefer my male interpreters wear a dress shirt, dress pants, and belt, while leaving the suit jacket and tie in the car. Sometimes, you are interpreting in situations where that isn't appropriate. I understand, a suit and tie can be culturally necessary when interpreting in formal or extreme business situations. If you do wear a suit, just remember to keep it monochromatic if possible, and if not, opt for colors that closely match; e.g.: a black suit jacket with a dark purple shirt and dark purple tie. Your consumers will love the great background and you will also look pretty snazzy.

Color Combos

Do the Deaf care? I posed this question to numerous Deaf consumers: "If an interpreter is wearing a dark vest over a light shirt, or a light dress shirt under a dark suit jacket, or a bright colored tank under a dark shirt, do you find that type of color combination an issue?" The resounding response was, "YES!" The Deaf who responded *never* said, "Oh, it isn't a problem." Everyone I questioned said that it was in fact a distraction. I hear a lot of light skinned female interpreters say, "I just want a pop of color." My response is said in love, but with gentle honesty, "Your wardrobe color choices don't need to be about your personal preferences, but about making your signs as accessible as possible for your consumers." That means we need to say goodbye to the white tank tops under our black shirts, bye to our red tank tops under our dark gray shirts, bye to our light/dark or dull/bright color conflicts in any setting, and we need to say adios to the visual noise. What's the message? Let's make using an interpreter a visually positive experience for our consumers.

...And What About?

Patterns are a problem, always. Obviously paisley is a "no-no," but any pattern, can cause a visual conflict which cannot be discounted:

- o Patterns: I can't even believe I have to say it, but YouTube and American television has convinced me it's necessary, so here it goes. **DON'T WEAR PATTERNS, *EVER!*** Male interpreters across the U.S. regularly wear ties with enormous patterns on them and claim it isn't distracting. Huh? On dresses, I have seen polka dots, and stripes, and swirls, and more! On shirts, the pain continues. Someone find me a brick wall to bang my head against! In the words of Nancy Reagan, "Just say no!"

- o Writing: It is never ok. If you are interpreting for Rascal Flatts and you thought a RF Tour T-shirt would be fine, think again!

- o Logos: In my fantasy world, I would never encourage any form of additives to your solid background. I do understand that sometimes they are required. If there is no escape, logos should be small images over the pocket area.

- Blocks of Color: Blocks of similar colors are clearly an issue too. If your hands cross multiple color tones, you are *NOT* considered to be wearing a solid background! One time, I brought in an interpreter for an outdoor concert. He arrived wearing a blue shirt... that is it was light blue on top, medium blue in the middle, and dark blue on bottom. I said, "Is that what you are interpreting in?" He said, "Well, it's BLUE!" Uh, dude, seriously? One color per garment, people.
- Lace: Some lace can possibly be a distraction. Even if your lace is in the appropriate color tone, still that pattern can effectually create too much visual noise. I wear lace, but I have to wear it with care and wisdom.

So today, let's say *goodbye* to your polka dots, say *adios* to your stripes, wave *arrivederci* to any wording, and let's add a final *au revoir* to any images on your person top or bottom (With the exception of a uniform with a required company logo on a pocket). And people, I say this in love, take the name tags off while you interpret. Ok, I feel better. Feeling cleansed. Happiness...

Clothing Additives & Accessories

Buttons can be a problem if they are shiny or an alternative color. Flaps can be an issue. Depending on the color, cloth tiers can be a distraction. They all can create "visual noise" for your consumers, and visual noise is something you want to avoid. A smooth

91

background or a relatively smooth background is always an interpreter's first choice. I always encourage my students to stop and think, "Does this draw attention from my hands and/or arms?" If the answer is "yes", leave it in the closet.

Are you Muslim? Opposing skin tones are still required for Muslim dress. I saw a dark skinned Muslim terp on the internet wear a black jilbab. Nope, not ok. The color rules don't lose their merit when you cross a religious barrier. However, that's not the only "yikes" we see among Muslim interpreters who dress in traditional Muslim attire. We need to take a moment and talk about your hijabs. I have seen some Muslim interpreters believe their shirts, pants or jilbabs should oppose their skin tone, but their hijabs are free game to be as funky as they want. Say it isn't so! Ladies, your hijabs count as clothing apparel, which means you need to keep them design free, and you need to keep the color opposing your skin tone. Don't break the rules. Again, your consumers will appreciate the consideration and your consumer's visual comfort does matter.

Clothing Length

I am 5' 1 ½" (believe me, at my height acknowledging that ½" is critical) which means I am a shrimp. Clothes don't fit me. Everything is too long. My shorts are capris, my arm holes can hang to my waist, regular skirts look like maxi-dresses, and there is one undeniable fact, my sleeves have driven more Deaf people crazy than anything else in my wardrobe. It took me years to realize how frustrating it was for my consumers, and the phrase, "roll up your sleeves" has been signed to me more than even, "hello" in my lifetime. So, vertically challenged people like me, roll up those sleeves or better yet buy ¾ length sleeves! The Deaf actually need to *SEE* your hands to understand what you are saying. I know, go figure. ::: head slap :::

Sleeve length isn't just a "short person" problem. All interpreters should ideally wear ½ or ¾ length sleeves to create a nice background for their hands and arms. Remember that the Deaf don't just look at your fingers; they look at your forearms as well. It's ideal to have both available for their seeing pleasure. Guys, that means that you may need to roll up your dress shirts at times. Sleeves won't stay up? Use a pin or a rubber band to keep them in place. Girls, we also need to make our forearms bear if possible. If your religion doesn't allow for your arms to show, then consider layering a tight skin colored top under a shorter elbow length opposing color so the Deaf again have the most effective color combination. What about sleeveless shirts? Sleeveless shirts and tanks are never an ideal option for interpreters. I know, half the interpreters in America wear sleeveless, but to create a significant solid background for your arms you need something on your upper arms. Don't shoot me. It might be hot, but even if you don't have floppy underarms (sadly, like yours truly), you need to keep in mind that your upper arm area needs to stay covered in order to create a clear and easy background for your signs. I know I have rocked the world of more than a few terps. I am just here to help! Stay with me.

Some interpreters succumb to open midriff fashions when they interpret. Your bellies should not be available for on the job observation. Even if you are interpreting a swim class where you wear a suit, I suggest laying off the bikini and opting for a full suit. The more coverage your body has, the better. On standard jobs, many ladies buy shirts which are an appropriate and professional length when their arms are hanging by their sides; however what they don't notice or realize to be an issue is when they lift their hands above their heads, surprise! Their bellies show. This is particularly obvious for light skinned Performance Interpreters. I might be Greek/Lebanese which means I look ethnic but the fact is that this belly has never seen the sun, and woo, if I wear a slightly shorter shirt, then lift my arms above my head for a dramatic sign on stage, the Deaf crowd will be subjected to a humanoid version of the surface of the sun. If your shirts are of questionable length, and can't pass the a clothing test where one throws the hands high above the head to evaluate belly blow-outs, it's a good idea to wear a tank top under them. It solves a slew of problems: no accidental midriff unveilings followed by the added protection of an undershirt if buttons were to pop open on a job.

Then there is the issue of skirt length. Ladies, the crowd doesn't need to see your "business". As professionals we first need to wear a skirt the proper length and then, in an act of kindness to our consumers, keep our legs together. One local interpreter missed this memo in her ITP. She wasn't a small woman, but apparently was wearing a small skirt. I was told she interpreted at a local venue for an hour with her legs wide open leaving a breathtaking display of her unmentionables. Apparently, many people in the first 10 rows were bothered by this unwanted demonstration of under fashion, and even tried to direct ushers to intervene judiciously. I don't think it worked. Ladies, you might have a recent, and nothing less than magnificent purchase from Victoria Secret, one that brings you great pride, but your audience doesn't need to know. Longer skirts and crossed legs are the key to happiness for most of your Deaf and Hearing consumers. Shorter skirts can be manageable in situations not involving a stage, but still need to be chosen and handled with care. Just remember, if you choose a skirt any shorter than a maxi-dress, those legs need to remain in a location where your audience feels compelled to look at your face rather than your nether regions.

What about the stage? Stages are tough. Platform and stage interpreting usually means that interpreters are placed 3 – 10 feet in the air. That often means a short skirt becomes a tempting target for a wandering eye. Remember the old adage, "Test it before you wear it"? That is even more critical in the interpreting world. If you wear the questionable skirt, stand on a chair, a bed, or stairs at home, ones which mimic the level of the stage, then ask a friend to confirm your under-display as you practice a bit of interpreting, you can usually discover rather quickly if you have adorned a skirt providing safety, or one posing great danger. No matter what, I strongly recommend any interpreter opting to wear any skirt, wear black undies, so accidental revelations become mistaken for shadows. Our goal? Limit attire which encourages curious gazes.

Clothes Bought Outside this Decade

If your clothes are looking rough, if they are faded and your blacks are now gray, your purples are turning a grayish mauve, your forest greens are now mossy green, please replace them. These days you can purchase a decent interpreting shirt for $10 at Wal-Mart. After a year or two of washes, shirts are often faded and look less than professional. I cringe when interpreters get their old black outfits on then go interpret a concert. Once in place, those stage lights hit their faded frocks and their blacks change to hazy grays, hazy browns, hazy reds, even hazy blues, and they look bad. Don't be the one who do that!

Certain materials hold color better. Polys hold black for years. If you can find clothes with a little spandex in them, they retain color better and move with you, so those are a nice option. Cottons, although far more comfortable, do fade over time. Look for clothes that are intensely dyed and don't look slightly faded when you buy them, as those won't last. I have a few shirts, which after 15 years, still look new, and others which need to be replaced within a year. Be attentive to your colors. Shop around. Don't always opt for the cheapest option. In addition, do what has been hard for me to do; let your clothes go when it's time. Your consumers will thank you!

Stilettos Anyone?

I am not Imelda Marcos (if you remember she had more than 3,000 pairs of shoes). I do like shoes, and being just barely over 5' tall means heels carry a soft spot in my heart. 5" heels knock my stunted frame up to the height of a "normal person," so I am all about a great pair of heels. (My ex-roommate/ex-boss is glowing as she reads this. She didn't like my tennis shoe phase.) Having said that, I can say the 5" heels sitting in my closet can be a recipe for disaster. One day I was working in the office when I got called to an emergency room assignment. Those go by really quickly, don't they? (More Sam sarcasm.) Of course, what was I wearing? Yep my 5" heels and Sam didn't bring her back-up shoes that day. I had to stand for five hours straight in those heels. By hour four, I was trying to shift my weight every which way just to relieve the pressure momentarily. It was a painful day. Shoe choices matter.

Shoes can be problematic for more reasons than just lack of comfort. Interpreters who wear Birkenstocks to medical or legal assignments can leave a less than professional impression. Interpreters who wear yellow shoes with their black outfits under the mistaken guise that adding a "pop of color" generates no distraction, have some re-evaluation to do. Some interpreters wear nice outfits then don scuffed-up old shoes. Confession: this was one of my previous faux pas. I wasn't donning my tennis shoes on assignments, but I never stopped to consider the impact of my shoes on my overall look. I thought, "What does it matter?" One day, the revelation hit; I looked at my shoes and realized they looked ridiculous with my dress pants. I was pretty disappointed in myself. We really need to pay more attention to our presentation, and that includes our feet. Appearances do matter.

Dressing Right for your Body Type

I hope to God when you read this book, I am a size 2, or even a size 6, but sadly as I write it, I am not. Not even close. Not even kinda close. I was a size 2 in Jr. High, for an hour or two. I have worn anything from a size 6 to a size 22 since I stopped growing (which we have established, didn't leave me very tall). I guess we could say I am a human weight yo-yo. The fact is the bigger I got, the more I had to pay attention to how I dressed.

I am known for being a Performance Interpreter. Give me a play or a concert and 10,000 people and I am a happy camper. However, with the stage comes stage lights, and stage lights are unforgiving. If you are more curvaceous than others, remember looser clothes are better. Some women don't want to wear loose apparel. Maybe they want to embrace their curves and they feel tighter clothes represent their personal style more effectively, or in some cases they just opt for tighter apparel because purchasing the next size up is not emotionally palatable. I get it! I have been there. I know it might be uncomfortable, but picking a larger size isn't a bad thing! Your identity isn't in your size; it's in you as a person, so give it a try. Here's the issue: tight clothing can draw emphasis to the rolls of our Plus Sized bodies. Trust me, I know! Sometimes a slightly more tailored fit is better in business settings, but often curvaceous terps draw emphasis *TO* rather than *AWAY* from their problem areas through their overly snug ensembles. Looser clothing allows for less pulling and stretching of the clothes, and removes emphasis on problem areas. Stage lights highlight the top of every roll leaving the bottom of every roll in shadow. Not pretty. Added perk: Deaf consumers, being so visually oriented, notice these bod issues twice as fast as Hearing consumers. Added added perk: Being blunt Deaf people, you might just get one that mentions it to you in a very inhibition-free way. Need an example? I have one. Many moons ago, I was interpreting in front of many hundreds of people, a number of them were Deaf, one was a friend of mine. This friendship could be the *ONLY* reason she is alive and well today. The minute my stage time came to a close, my friend walked straight up to me and before even uttering a "Thank you for interpreting," she said, "People your size shouldn't wear a shirt like that." Wow, cool, thanks. I have lost a lot of weight since then, but clearly what I wore, mattered. Any type of interpreting lends a need for appropriate dress and wearing the appropriate fit. Never be embarrassed to make changes. As you change let your wardrobe morph with you, and find ways to present yourself in the best manner possible.

Men! You thought you were free from this conversation. No, you are not. If you have worked years on that beer gut of yours, make sure you buy shirts that can either be tucked into your pants and remain tucked in, or buy shirts that are meant to be worn outside of your pants. Your gut matters just as much as ours. Guys, when you buy a shirt, make sure the buttons don't look strained, and you can move in it freely. Like the ladies, the goal is to look professional and not emphasize any of your body issues. With the right size and color, gut or no gut, you can look quite snazzy. If you dress right for your body type, the result leads to far less distraction, and it offers the potential for more focus on what people came to see, your signs.

Thin people! You are not excluded. Some girls wear very tight clothes with the mindset that they are skinny, so the fit doesn't matter. It matters. You might be thin, but an incredibly tight shirt on anyone breeds attention.

Ladies with bigger chests, I am not sure what happens in America, but I have been secretly pulled aside at more workshops than I can count, and asked to teach on how interpreters should not reveal too much of the girls. All across the U.S. female interpreters must be flashing America because their friends and co-workers definitely want this topic addressed in their honor. So, for all of your attendees who secretly begged me to bring up the benefits of coverage, this paragraph is for you. First, ladies who are blessed up above, we need the keep the girls hidden. I know they are powerful tools for getting attention, but on the job we need people's eyes above the headlights. Interpreters should strive to avoid distraction, and a voluminous chest out for the world to see is definitely a distraction. Secondly, more skin equals less background. You all know how much I love a complete and solid background for your signs. Cloth means coverage so skimpy is the enemy. One final note to the blessed ladies, danger is something you want to avoid, so remember button down shirts can look and feel a little more strained with a noteworthy upper half. I know this from experience. Some ladies have a less endowed build, which does quite well with button down shirts. My "girls," however, like to try and make an appearance through any and all available flaps and holes. Shirts with few or no buttons I have found to be far safer. These days some shirts are cut more appropriately for women with big chests and if you find a shirt which won't pull and tug, go for it.

Dressing right for your body type can mean attention to coverage, size, cut, and style. None of us are perfect at this. I have bought something and thought it looked great for a week, then realized it didn't work for me. Experiment, ask questions of your friends and consumers, consider a stylist consultation, and have fun being the beautiful people that you are, with all your individual shapes and sizes.

Dressing for the Environment

Wear clothes that fit the environment in which you are interpreting. If you are in a doctor's office, opt for something more professional than a broom skirt or rolled up beach capris. Make sure the colors look like new. If you are interpreting for the governor, wear something more formal than a t-shirt. If you are interpreting at a church, you may want to dress more conservatively. If you are interpreting for a children's camp, a t-shirt and shorts might be just the ticket. Remember, you are there to fit into an environment not distract from it. Little decisions like that make a big difference for our consumers.

Years ago a Nashville based musician growing in fame had a Deaf family member who was coming to visit. He asked me to spend some time with him, which of course I agreed to do. Had I only known! His family member came to my evening sign language class as a guest speaker. He seemed ok, at first. He wasn't an amazing speaker, but he got to know some students in town and they of course loved meeting a Deaf person. He asked me to interpret for him at an event which would happen immediately after the class. The class ended late so I wasn't sure what I was getting into, but said "Sure! Glad to help." I owed him one. (Sam, next time, ask more questions.) I asked him if I was appropriately dressed; he said I looked perfect. (Sam, next time, remember, ask more questions.) An hour later, we arrived on site, late at night, me with my short hair, pants, and sporting 2 lbs. of Cover Girl on my face. As we walked in, I felt a bit out of place when I looked around and we were apparently walking into a meeting with women dressed in long jean skirts, no makeup, and every head featuring hair down to the waist. Uh, yeah, I looked just a LITTLE out of place. Yikes! One-by-one the entire group slowly turned their heads and looked at me. I was incredibly embarrassed. He apparently didn't notice. The rest of the story is hilarious, very long, very dramatic, and would breed a hug from you, I am sure. In summation, after 3 ½ - 4 hours of interpreting all by myself, I walked out of there with a scowl, no energy, emergent irritation, a bout of complete humiliation, and the invariable knowledge that Sam needs to learn to *ASK MORE QUESTIONS*. I never saw him again. I am pretty content with that.

What was tragic about that event besides my obvious need for a team interpreter? My appearance caused negative attention to be drawn to me.

Interpreters are supposed to blend and breed unity. I failed, because I didn't ask more questions. Many interpreters believe that a classic black shirt and pants provide the necessary neutrality for interpreting. Sometimes classic black is what *causes* attention and becomes a visual contradiction. At a Britney Spears concert, a sexier outfit would be more appropriate to blend with the environment. The goal is to be environmentally equivalent and appropriate.

"Environmentally Appropriate" can mean a long skirt at the meeting I interpreted. It can mean a shorter tighter skirt when interpreting for the musical *Chicago*. At a country concert it likely means jeans. In a court room, a suit would be ideal. For a community play, a costume could be fitting. For track practice, you can't go wrong with a polo. "Appropriate" has different meanings in different venues. As interpreters, dressing appropriately is critical, and very much appreciated by our consumers.

– The Outer You –
Coiffing and Clawing

It seems so logical, and yet apparently it's not. Hair and nails do matter. Interpreters allow for a wide variety of lazy allotments in their lives. I can't tell you the number of interpreters that I have met who need a bit of help in this area. I understand hair is not the easiest subject. My Office Manager tells me that in humidity I look like the Obama Chia Pet. It's true. My Greek/Lebanese head loves to go "fro" in bad weather, and keeping it under control sometimes is a flat out act of God. I have made some good, and on occasion, some bad choices in the hair area. Where my mistakes end, other people's errors begin, so let's discuss hair, and I promise to come clean and admit the error of my ways.

First, *do your hair*. I know, this is a shock, but many people don't consider it a priority. Sadly, somehow, this little tip eluded me in my younger days. I slept so little that I took very little time with my hair in the mornings. I sometimes showed up to early morning college interpreting assignments with wet hair. Granted, it takes a very long time for my hair to dry, but looking back, that was a bad call. I should have cared more about how rough I looked with a wet head in the mornings. So those were not winning moments for me. I have had to chat with interpreters about brushing their hair. Grab the brush and tame the coif! Secondly, if even effort isn't going to help, *get a NEW "do"!* Sporting a bun pulled so tight that the capillaries in your eyeballs bulge? Maybe not. 3" of gray topping 10" of black? Not ideal. When people see your head do they relive memories of their childhood photos? Maybe another do would be better. We are the representatives of our consumers, which means our presentation needs a little time, and a little effort.

So let's redefine once non-existent hair goals. In summary, remember a few tips. Look respectable. A mullet is out, so let it go. Hair brushing is in, so give it a shot. If your hairdo makes you look like an 1800's schoolmarm or a zombie-like serial killer, you might want to rethink the "do". Create a look which is attractive, not terrifying. Avoid colors that are outside the norm or are incredibly distracting. Pink, blue, and purple are not so great for the average interpreting assignment. Pink hair when interpreting for Nicki Minaj, that's a whole other story. Go for it. The goal is to think *blend* not *distract*. If she is in a pink phase, it can work. In Performance settings, I suggest an appearance similar to the artists (singers) or talent (actors) you are representing. For example, if you are interpreting for Carrie Underwood, do more than your standard personal style; consider using temporary hair extensions for the night. If you are interpreting for Cher, consider teasing your hair and going for volume. And yes, if you are interpreting for Nicki, pick whatever crazy color she is sporting at the time, I could care less. That's a lie, I care some. If you *do* decide to go more "extreme" with your hair, maybe think about maintaining some limitations. If Nicki is in a pink phase, maybe just dye the tips pink, and get the flavor of her crazy hair color, but without as much distraction. The Deaf are visual individuals so anything that makes a visually cohesive environment is an effective additive to your personal presentation. However, normally even slightly less shocking colors can still be too intense. Extremely bright reds or white whites can be a bit stark and draw too much attention for a Mental Health job. Just remember, we are on assignment to represent OTHERS, not ourselves, so try and bring some visual consistency and neutrality to the table when possible.

Quick note: when on assignments, leave your hair alone! Girls, we have all done it. I know interpreters across the country with this issue, and for some it is nearly an addiction. Keep finger/hair interaction to a minimum while on the job. Don't pull it behind your ear every 30 seconds, don't twist it constantly, don't pull it behind your shoulders, then in front, then back again. Leave it alone. Every time you play with it, the message is broken.

"So the professor was
[pulling hair behind her ear]
talking with her brother
[pulling hair behind her ear]
who was living in Ft. Lauderdale, FL
[pulling hair behind her ear]."

Do you enjoy reading it? Watching it is worse.

As for nails, think natural. Into mani-pedis? If you spend money on acrylics, it's ok if they are not too long. However remember, clicking acrylic nails can be distracting, so no clicking your nails while on the job. Painting your nails bold colors is an interpreter no-no. Do you assume all interpreters know and abide by this? Let me burst that little bubble. Do you know how many people I see come directly from assignments and arrive at my workshops with crazy colored nails? It's astonishing! Light skinned? Opting for a reasonable length in an American or French manicure is an acceptable alternative to natural nails. If painting a solid color, light tans or light pinks will do. Dark skinned? Opting for a color similar to your skin tone is fabulous when paying for that manicure.

Your nails do matter, more than you think! One Deaf individual pulled me aside at a workshop in the Mid-West and complained about an interpreter who had injured his nail. The discolored area made the consumer think a bug was flying in the room. He told me he would have preferred the interpreter wear a Band-Aid over his finger rather than interpret with a discolored wound. Interesting, isn't it? So people, keep those nails on the shorter side, keep them painted appropriately. Let me say it once again, and again sound like that critically needed broken record, appearance matters.

Face Painting

I have run into a number of interpreters who hate makeup. Hate it. I mean, at their core they want nothing to do with it. I have also met interpreters who would accept the use of makeup, but historically they have had no idea how to apply it. In addition, I have run across interpreters who do not wear makeup for religious reasons, or because they feel it defies the generally accepted physical expression of their orientation. I know makeup is often loved, but other times detested by the masses. Surprisingly, people can get belligerent when discussing makeup. At one workshop on the East Coast, I suggested people wear eye shadow on stage to define their eyes and one woman nearly became violent. It's just makeup! Having said that, let's talk about face painting a bit. If you are one of those pugnacious ladies... keep breathing and keep smiling. This is a short section.

If you are not against wearing makeup for religious reasons, I want to talk to you. Makeup helps. It can be as simple as mascara and lip gloss, or it can be a full make-over every morning, but defining your face is a positive thing. Deaf people gather an enormous amount of information from the face. Eyes that are defined pop which allows for a consumer to quickly and easily engage with the interpreter. Lip gloss or lipstick, even Burt's Bees organic tinted lip balm makes a huge difference for the Deaf. I have had interpreters argue with me about this at workshops. (Interpreters argue? Say it isn't so!) I was teaching a workshop in the Southeast, and clearly one attendee thought I was insane for suggesting ASL interpreters wear some form of color on their lips. She piped up to prove me wrong, and asked the opinion of one of the Deaf evaluators in the room, a woman who was a very well-respected ASL user in the area. The interpreter stopped the entire workshop to pose the question, expecting my theory would be shot down. It didn't work out quite like she had planned. The Deaf lady looked at her, grinned, nodded her head vigorously and said, "She's right. It helps." Did she think I was lying? I laugh at the way interpreters get volatile over silly things. I often work with starving Deaf children in Mexico, children who are beaten and abused and even sold into the sex trade because they are poor and Deaf. With a world full of truly serious battles to fight, interpreters in America are going to become irate over the suggestion of lip-gloss? Perspective people! So, the truth is, a little color goes a long way, and just because the Deaf don't demand it of each other, doesn't mean they don't prefer it in their interpreters.

What are the facial features which are well served with a little appliqué? Define your eyes. It really engages the Deaf. If you are relatively anti-makeup, opt for at least mascara and eyeliner. If you love makeup, pop onto YouTube and check out one of the 10,000 lessons on how to do your eye makeup. Lips are a good thing to define. Again, even ASL users watch your mouth more than you realize. Throw on a little color and they will enjoy how much easier it is to gather information from your mouth. Your cheeks define the shape of your face. If you love makeup this is an easy one to add to the mix. Cheek color draws attention to the center of your face and that visual draw is great for interpreters. Want to lose a few pounds? Throw some bronzer under your jaw line and along your hair line. Just remember, YouTube is full of tips and tricks for doing your makeup, so take a few moments to watch the videos and play a little!

What kind of makeup do I suggest you *NOT* wear? Sometimes interpreters get a bit over zealous.

Some people can get away with it, many cannot. If a very dark skinned interpreter wears eye shadow which extends from lashes to brow, and her color choices are incredibly bold like gold, fuchsia, white, or teal, it can become a distraction. I have seen ladies do this, and I can't look away from their eye lids. I forget they even have eyes. I just keep staring at their lids in some kind of mesmerized trance: TURQUOISE.... TURQUOISE... TUUUUURRRQUOISE! That isn't an ideal reaction from your consumers. Your makeup should only enhance, not be the center of attention.

Who can *NEVER* go without makeup? Stage Interpreters! Performance interpreters under stage lights desperately need makeup. In some cases, standard makeup is fine. In some cases, stage makeup is even better. Stage lighting will flatten your face and make your features disappear in a second. Again, YouTube is a powerful weapon in the hands of an interpreter, so get on there and play around a bit. Your consumers will thank you!

Bedazzling You

I am sure that your 2K diamond ring is beautiful, but if Deaf people need to wear sunglasses when you interpret, you might need to "de-bedazzle" yourself. Your watch or necklace might be lovely, but do they attract unwanted attention? Whatever jewelry you wear, make sure it doesn't tear the eyes away from what is being said. An interpreter walked into my office recently with an enormous black costume jewelry necklace. I know what she was thinking, "It is black, isn't it?" Yeah, it was black, but it was *HUGE!* Any jewelry that draws significant attention from the face is considered inappropriate for interpreters. In Performance settings, make sure your jewelry fits the genre of the performers you are emulating, and remember, on stage, everything shiny, gets shinier! Keep in mind, what you often think bears little relevance, does in fact impact the comprehension or distraction level of your consumers.

Body Art Modifications

Ah yes, welcome to the 21st Century! There is nothing we can't do to our bodies. Today interpreters come packed full of modifications. Tattooing is not limited to arms and legs but people now tattoo their faces and corneas. Simple piercings have given way to plugs and eyelets, tapers and stretching, and a vast array of labrets. Where there was once just a small image placed on the body now there is scarification, branding and tongue bifurcation (which just all looks like it hurts way too much for me). So now that we can do anything to our bodies, where should the line be drawn?

I remember once a Deaf professional, who I am sure many of you know and love, came to me and griped profusely that his interpreter, did not represent him well in business meetings because he had an unkempt ponytail. That was just a ponytail, and the consumer was infuriated. Our personal style affects how people view and interact with our Deaf clientele. It's just a fact. You may not like it, but it's not going to change, at least not any time soon. If an interpreter shows up at a corporate meeting and has a snake tattoo down his arm, or a skull implant under the skin of his hand, or a stretched ear, the Hearing consumers in the room can often inadvertently allow those images to reflect on their perspective of the Deaf consumer. In some cases, it can even become a tremendous distraction. There's a general rule of thumb that interpreters should live by. If it's a part of the body which can be viewed by others, leave it alone. Don't tattoo it, implant it, stretch it, and/or pierce it in an unusual and generally culturally non-discrete manner. What no one can see, knock yourself out. I have heard from multiple consumers that discretion is their preference. Let's say you are only going to interpret at body art conventions, as your primary employment is as a professional graphic designer. In that case, everyone at those body art cons will probably think it's cool to sport whatever art and modifications you desire, so go for it. Well, you still might want to avoid tattooing your face blue, corneas red, and implanting horns, but you get the idea. However, those of us who have to interpret in schools, medical settings, corporate or religious meetings, legal proceedings, and mental health appointments, probably need to keep our bodies looking unaltered. Also remember, before you decide to get any modifications, remember one little unquestionable truth: the field you interpret in today, is not necessarily the field you will be interpreting in tomorrow.

Can alterations do more than distract? YES! For example, it's rather obvious if you have a bifurcated tongue, your consumer is going to notice and probably be distracted while you are interpreting. A tongue that is moving in two opposing directions is noticeable. If you are an interpreter with a tattoo of a snake down your arm, and you walk into a meeting where the consumer has Ophidiophobia (a fear of snakes), then you could send your consumer into a panic attack at the word, "Hello." If you get called to a meeting with a Jewish consumer and you have a swastika on your neck, it might cause a problem, or two, or three. If you are interpreting for an individual who is quite squeamish, and you have an extreme piercing, like, let's say, an uncovered corset piercing down your back, you can do more than draw attention, you can make someone physically ill.

"But I want to get body art and body modifications! It's my body and if someone has a problem with it, it is *THEIR* problem, not mine!" Sounds like a good platform for change doesn't it? However, we forget one thing, that as interpreters, our job isn't to represent ourselves; we are there to represent our consumers. A lot of fields breed limitations. A surgeon cannot have long manicured nails for health reasons and functionality concerns. The teeth of a dentist cannot be missing or rotten, that's just bad advertising. As sign language interpreters our presentation must maintain an element of neutrality and obscurity so we can blend into the environments for which we are called to interpret.

"But I already have an obvious tattoo!" Cover it. An obvious tattoo is not a heart the size of a dime on the back of someone's neck, hidden under the hair, but a sleeve tattoo, yep, a tad obvious. Don't hate me, but I suggest in order to keep the neutrality going, obvious alterations and art should be covered or removed. If you have a skull implant on your arm, have them place it on your back where it can be covered by your shirt, or exposed when desired. If you have plugs in your earlobes, you may want to remove them for assignments and if extremely significant stretching has occurred, then consider using a Band-Aid to twist and hold the stretched portion up to the base of the ear. If you have a tattoo on your forearm, and the weather makes sleeves less enticing, go to Sephora in JCPenney and grab some water resistant tattoo concealer and cover that sucker up. You can jump on Amazon or eBay and buy a tatjacket to cover tattoos which are extreme and too large to be hidden with the application of specialized makeup. We have to remember, the Deaf are more visual than the Hearing, and their attention can be drawn to your body art or body modifications even faster than a Hearing person. As your job is never to distract from the interpretation or the environment, if your art will do that, honor the consumers who would be affected by it and manage it as needed. In standard interpreting environments, your presentation should have an element of neutrality.

What now?

One or two of you right now are likely "fighting mad" as they say in the South. You like things the way you have been doing them and I come along, telling you to change your wardrobe, your hair, your makeup, etc! I know more than one person will be texting a friend during this chapter and asking if they agree, but I am going to go out on a limb here and say that if you have to defend it, it likely should not be done. The fact is these basic standards were created for the benefit of our consumers. They are not in place with the purpose of torturing the interpreters; they are there to make the experience of using an interpreter easier and more effective. Personally, I think if people fight against these standards they are focused on one thing, themselves. If a few changes can be made to our presentation so that the experience of being Deaf and using an interpreter is a little less taxing, then why shouldn't we want to do those things? My wardrobe looks like that of a funeral director, but I will live, and hopefully my consumers will live happier.

TERZIS' TIPS!

DON'T SWEAT IT!

Do you sweat? Or perspire? Or glisten? There are some great products to keep the perspiration to a minimum. Any time interpreters have to interpret outdoors, interpret vigorously for an extended period of time, or if they interpret on stages under stage lights, they sweat, or perspire, or glisten. Whatever. Is this you? Wait! There is hope! You can help stop the outpouring of those pesky skin based secretions! How?

Mary Kay makes a product called Oil Mattifier. This is a great product for reducing the oil your skin produces. It also reduces the sweat you produce. This is a great product to have in hand! It works especially well for your standard interpreting assignments. Pop onto Mary Kay's webpage or find a local consultant and give it a try.

There is also a product called, "No Sweat," or "ProFace Skin Prep Pro." Do you have a rigorous interpreting job? Do you interpret in humidity? Do you interpret for outdoor sports? Do you interpret for concerts and theatrical performances? This product is for you! It handles more aggressive environments. It reduces the sweat, the perspiration, and the glistening you produce while you are working. It can be used to keep you from looking like you are melting in front of your consumers. Just apply it under your makeup and you will look better, longer. (I sound like a commercial, don't I?) Give it a try! You can find it online.

Use at your own risk.

FINDING THE LINE IN THE SAND

Boundaries are difficult to manage. They are influenced by our moral, religious, and cultural preferences, our personal securities or insecurities, our interpreting environments, ITP background or lack thereof, our consumers, age, or the type of day we are having. Boundaries can change daily, and maintaining them is one of the hardest things for an interpreter to accomplish. Speaking to this is hard because my "take" on boundaries may not be your "take," and that can be a challenging place to have a conversation. There are entire books on the subject of personal boundaries, and websites have dedicated countless pages to their explanation. I am devoting one brief chapter to the topic. Some people will likely think my perspectives are not strong enough, and others will think they are too strong. I tend to have a pretty "middle of the road" view on what professional boundaries should be. Let's delve into boundaries and take a look at some different perspectives on what they could and should look like.

– What Drives Sam –

Before we launch into this section, I thought it would be good to understand one of the guiding factors for my boundaries, my Christianity. Someone just threw this book out the window! Christian! EEK! Not in the liberal interpreting world! Yep, I am one of *THOSE* people. I believe in God, Jesus... the works. If you are now in the middle of a panic attack, hang in there. I know the Christian church isn't perfect, and Christians come in all forms, including some less than inspiring versions. I need to confess, I believe in church and the Bible; I believe in heaven, hell, salvation, the whole nine yards, and I am a Californian! If you made it past my first declaration, but have broken into hives at that last God remark, grab the ointment and keep reading. I know it's unpopular to be a Christian in the professional interpreting world. I always appreciate it when professional interpreters still love and respect me after they find out that I am one of those "holy rollers". (I wish we could insert sound effects in books because that would have been a fabulous place for a scream.) I have to say, my Christianity has guided a lot of my decisions. Keep breathing. Grab oxygen if necessary. I will explain.

You see, every day I walk into an assignment and think one thing, "How can I make a difference, here and now?" I believe as a Christian my job is in part to leave this world a better place than what it was when I found it. Sometimes that means making people laugh at a workshop, sometimes it means encouraging people when they cry, sometimes it means listening, sometimes it means confronting, and I honestly believe for me it means providing a quality service for my consumers. Whatever it means, it means every day I don't just "do" a job, I try to make a difference while I am on a job. Obviously, I can't hug a client or start praying out loud for someone when they are being told they have a terminal illness, but I can make the experience of being Deaf and using an interpreter the best it possibly can be. I still believe wholeheartedly that all interpreters, even us darn Christians, should abide by the CPC (or Code of Ethics for us old folks). Our office has strict perspectives on maintaining the tenets of the CPC. The CPC defines things so well. However, as a Christian, I can't just maintain the CPC goal of equality and accessibility, but I have to look at Biblical goals as well. The result is that I don't want to just do the job, I want to do it with a smile, and without added character traps I see interpreters fall into. Many interpreters might feel only the accuracy of an interpreted message serves as the defining factor for a success. I know numerous interpreters with that perspective, Christian and Non-Christian alike. Though, I think as Christians, limiting your attention to simply the provision of the information, without the consideration of your inevitable positive or negative influence on a situation, is a tad harder to justify. Do I feel my Christianity gives me a license to hold the hands of a client on a job when they receive bad news? No. Do I believe that it requires me to make the experience as painless as possible through the quality of service I provide, and through the manner with which I provide it? YES! What I do is critical. In my opinion, *HOW* I do the job is equally as critical. In the end, I want every client to leave an assignment feeling like I am a professional and feeling like they had a wonderful experience in working with me. Have my personal boundaries ever been stretched? A few times, for reasons which I considered to be for the greater good. Clearly, I believe in abiding by the CPC, that's a no brainer. Sometimes there are those obscure "unwritten rules" of interpreting which, as interpreters, we have to look at a little deeper as we draw our own personal line in the sand. Before we dive in to the delineation of those boundaries as I personally define them, I need to have a chat with my people.

– A Note to the "Bible Thumpers" –

Let me just talk to the four other Christians in the professional interpreting world. Or is it five? Well, anyway, you know who you are. You are an example of Christ every minute you are on the job. Your smile matters. Your heart for people matters. No, you are not walking in with a t-shirt which says, "Jesus is Lord," but you are supposed to exemplify His love for others. Put your seatbelts on "thumpers," I say this in love, but it needs to be said. If you are a Christian and copping an attitude with your agencies, consumers, or team interpreters, knock it off. If you are moody, knock it off.

If you are a complainer, knock it off. If you are arrogant, knock it off. If you are defensive, knock it off. If you have let the job make you cynical, knock that off too. I could go on, but I will refrain. Be the example every day. Practice your signing. Practice your voicing. Dress with care. Be professional. Show love to your team interpreters (no matter how much you are tempted to physically abuse them when they get combative with you), and don't judge them for any reason. Provide a quality service to your consumers. We should never give people a reason to question our skill, our integrity, our professionalism, our attitudes, etc. Be your absolute best in every possible way. Doing that will make an impact, I promise! If you are one of the elusive five, shoot me an email, it's always nice to feel like I am not alone on this journey.

OK, soap box edict concluded. (Well, actually this entire book is one big soap box, isn't it?) Let's get back to the original box I jumped on in this chapter, those beloved boundaries.

(Congrats! You survived that section!)

– To Socialize or Not to Socialize –
– That is the Question! –
Extreme Professional Distance

There is a looming perspective on interpreter boundaries which states that interpreters should not socialize with the Deaf Community. The theory states that socializing with individuals who could become your consumers can produce a relationship, which would breach the distance interpreters have to maintain to keep neutrality and anonymity in play. I understand this perspective completely. I even partially agree with it. So let's break it down. Let's label this "Extreme Professional Distance". It has valid considerations. Let's look at some of the theoretical positives of this philosophy:

- More success at neutrality

  If the consumer and you are completely unacquainted, he or she is "just" a consumer and maintaining emotional separation becomes easier.

- More anonymity

  There is less opportunity for post assignment interaction as you will be less likely to cross paths on a social level at a later time.

- More freedom for emotional detachment

  If the interpreter is placed in a position where there is potential to be emotionally affected by an assignment, a lack of history or relationship provides for greater ease and less tertiary influences when relaying the mutual message.

All of this makes perfect sense doesn't it? Nonetheless, there are a few speed bumps which I find myself rumbling over along the way. First, there is an irrefutable truth that for an interpreter to embrace the constant evolution of the language, to understand the idiosyncrasies of the language, to improve fluency, and even to rev up after a hiatus, socialization is ideal, and dare I say, required. We develop our natural language skills by using the language, seeing the language, and interacting with the language in natural settings. The most basic of examples indicating a clear discrepancy between native and non-native Signers can be easily grasped by remarks from the community. I often see statements such as, "She signs like an Interpreter" compared to, "She signs like a Deaf person." This is a primary reason for encouraging socialization when considering language development. The Deaf themselves define a difference between the two styles of communication. If you are a professional interpreter, you likely know what I am talking about. Interpreters who primarily focus their efforts on interpreting alone have a formality to the style of their presentation, sometimes there is a subtle awkwardness, and there is frequently a definitive difference between their language production compared to that of their Deaf consumers. I see it quite regularly. Interpreters who clearly maintain a strict standard of "Extreme Professional Distance," who limit their personal socialization with the Deaf, will present songs, dialogues, stories, etc., with a decreased level of natural expression. Accuracy can also additionally affected. Does it matter? They are still getting the information out, right? Yes, they are. It's a lot like Google Translation Software, which works, and often works well, but it is not as effective as having a human translate what is said from a native perspective. Again, this is not a condemnation of that choice or of the signing success of someone who chooses to remain distant. There is a truth though that socialization with the Deaf brings that native, "human" touch to our translations. In verbal translation circles, native translations are always considered more effective. Interpreters, at least at the beginning of their careers, often strive for this natural fluid style, then later turn towards a more formalized, "interpreter like" presentation as their skills and experience advance. I honestly think we need to get back to that goal of creating visually indigenous interpretations. Spoken language interpreters still do make it a priority as they emphasize the development of native grammar, lexicon, and accent use. Why have we turned away from that? Some say, "We haven't", and then want to cite examples, but I travel the country and see it everywhere. I have, at the time of writing this book, taught workshops in 19 states. I have witnessed this stylized presentation in all 19. I think this turning from a natural linguistic expression has happened, in part, with the advancement of this "Extreme Professional Distance" theory.

A developing native accent and presentation skills are a good enough reason to promote socialization, but there are more linguistic based reasons to keep socialization on the table. When you socialize with the Deaf you develop local colloquialisms, you learn to alter your speed and style to match your adjusting locale, you learn to modify your presentation to match the types of consumers in your area, and you learn more natural methods of communication through personal interaction with native speakers. All of these attributes are incredibly beneficial for interpreters in the field. Let's take it further. Improved expression leads to improved consumer comprehension. I see interpreters all the time who present what is seemingly an acceptable interpretation for a particular type of Deaf Consumer, yet often the consumer struggles to comprehend what is interpreted. The interpreter has a certificate, he/she has those all-important quantifiable letters following his/her name, so what's the problem? What these interpreters sometimes don't have is the unique ability to word something in a manner which is more palatable for certain types of consumers. In the end, comprehension is lost. I think a loss of linguistic effectiveness becomes an identifiable concern, and it does breed a positive outlook on the argument toward socialization.

We have established that socialization impacts our linguistic abilities, but this concept is only one notable overall reason to pursue more active relationships with the community. Another is *trust*! Trust is often fostered out of relationship. I found many Deaf individuals do not trust interpreters. Often times, the ones that don't, find some solace in using an interpreter who socializes with the community. I saw this first hand at one point in my career. A particular Deaf individual I knew, refused to use and/or trust interpreters. This particular Deaf consumer was clearly the type of consumer who desperately needed an interpreter with them for important interactive activities, so I saw it as a travesty, knowing the limited communication which would ensue without intervention. I encouraged that individual to use interpreters, and to call our company when needed. When a call came in I was shocked, but thrilled. I hoped that maybe we could redeem the years of suspicion which had clearly been formulated in the mind of that consumer. I personally took the assignment, and I worked at building trust with all my might. I made sure, no matter how exhausted or uncomfortable I became over the course of the following hours, I would keep a smile. Eventually, when we were both worn emotionally and mentally, the consumer looked over at me and smiled and said with incredible tenderness and appreciation, "You are so sweet." It came out of nowhere. Something changed for that individual that day, and it happened because trust was built. That trust didn't start with an advertisement about our company's policies, a web video, or the maintenance of professional distance on the job; it started with my being involved in the community then was backed with a positive experience. Had that consumer not had the initial community interaction, there would have been no call for an interpreter, no chance for success or failure, and likely, continuing communicative disasters.

I had another incident come up with trust not long ago. Earlier this year I was invited to a Deaf Community party. I went, and somehow the topic of how I became an interpreter surfaced. 18 years in this town and no one had asked me that question, so I confess, I was shocked. It led to a nice conversation about my personal story, my experiences, their perspectives of interpreters, etc. Another interpreter's name was mentioned, someone who once had been a close personal friend. I suddenly saw a look of hurt come over their faces. They said, "She doesn't socialize with us anymore." I saw how, not one, but multiple women in the group still carried the emotional burden of one of their Hearing friends leaving them. It had been years, many years, since she had interacted with them! I was completely shocked. I saw, though, how important our relationships were to the community, and in that moment I realized that her departure and distance bred distrust. They talked about other interpreters that day, and they would follow their comments with, "but she doesn't socialize with us," or "she just works for so-and-so." Wow. This random interaction drove home the truth that it mattered whether or not interpreters were a part of their world. I am not saying every local Deaf Community has the same expectations. I have noticed that a number of large metropolitan areas tend to be a little more focused on interpreters serving as tools and that interaction may not carry the weight it does in other parts of the country. For most areas of the U.S., trust stems from three elements: time, interaction and experiences. The more trustworthiness an interpreter can offer to an assignment, the better.

We can all agree trust is a good starting point for interpreting assignments. Let's grab our shovels one more time and dig even further into a few personal comparisons. Here are a few analogies to consider. Imagine being a virgin, and Deaf, and needing to visit an OBGYN for your first girly exam. If your "hoo-hoo" was being exposed in such a vulnerable environment with an interpreter present, wouldn't you want to trust that interpreter on every level possible? What if you were being interviewed by an investigator about a sex crime committed against you? Wouldn't you want to know the interpreter relaying that information is kind, safe, and trustworthy? What if you just won the lottery and you were required to attend a meeting and sign paperwork regarding your newfound funds. Wouldn't you want the interpreter present to be more than merely skilled at financial terms, but rather an interpreter you could trust implicitly with the information being expressed? What if you were admitting to someone for the first time that you were a Star Trek fan, wouldn't you...? Well, let's skip that example. When dealing with raw, vulnerable, or extremely confidential information, often, it's the truly trustworthy interpreter who makes the cut. Trust doesn't come with credentials. Maybe it should, but it doesn't. If my personal business was about to be laid bare, especially if I myself LITERALLY was about to be laid bare, you bet I would want to be sure the person expressing that information a) communicated well on my behalf, b) behaved in a professional manner, c) had a good personality, and d) was someone I could trust implicitly. That's my opinion, and it is an opinion held by many consumers. I didn't say all consumers, because people are people, they are diverse, and some Deaf consumers just want you to do your job and go home. That's great. However for the many consumers who want or need more, an additional validation for the argument encouraging socialization is woven into the tapestry of our careers.

Those are some benefits of socialization, but let's remember, I said there were positives to the "Extreme Professional Distance" philosophy. How do we manage the situation if there are positives for both distance *and* socialization? You figure out what's best for you, your consumers, your agency, and your locale. As I said in the beginning of this section, the manifestation of each of our perspectives is both unique and individualized. It can also be ever changing. After decades in this field, I of course have had to define my personal boundaries in somewhat of a conclusive manner. "How?" Might you ask? I know the temptation will be to put on critical hats and start picking apart my philosophies like a ravenous buzzard on a lifeless carcass. Before we go *there*, let's keep in mind, I am merely expressing *MY* perspectives as they exist today. They may change as I change, our field changes, my residence changes, or those with whom I interact changes, etc. For now, here is "Sam's

Interactive Boundary System" or SIBS as I call it. (Mind you, I only started calling it that about 10 seconds ago, but it sounds official doesn't it?)

Intimate Relationships

If I have an intimate relationship with a consumer in advance (e.g.: dear friend) I will superficially chat with them on breaks or after the assignment. I *attempt* to always keep topics emotion free. I usually let them know, "For the course of this assignment we are not friends, I am just your interpreter. We get to be friends again at [insert time] once we leave here. For now, I am just here as your interpreter." Usually, I never have to repeat the speech again. They handle it very well, and rarely has one of these consumers even brought up my presence at an assignment once completed. It has been a very effective way to maintain personal boundaries.

Casual Relationships

If I know the consumer well but only have a casual relationship with him/her, I usually don't chat with him/her during assignment breaks or after unless about a non-personal topic (e.g.: "It looks like we might have tornados tomorrow"). Often, I won't chat at all. I feel out the consumer and figure out his/her expectations. My first option/preference is never to interact personally with a consumer while on the job, but some individuals find that rude, so I will, on occasion, if it remains superficial.

No Relationship

If I am not familiar with the consumer, I generally will not interact with them outside of the standard interpreting needs while on assignment. I still emote, "Friendly Sam," and draw a decisive line.

These boundaries have given me great success. I can maintain all kinds of interactive relationships with Deaf individuals and also keep margins with which everyone has felt comfortable.

– Sticking Your Big Toe Over the Line –

Clearly, I did not leave an ITP and five minutes later have a fabulous well defined, individually customized, radically founded perimeter to my professional life. If you claim to have that straight out of an ITP you are fibbing... a lot. So when have I bent SIBS? One time, in the beginning of my career, I had a student who weighed heavily on my heart. I could see the student's depression, and I could see that the rest of the world wasn't noticing what was happening in his/her life. I could see the extreme loneliness. At the time, I was also working under the "Conduit Model" of interpreting where interpreters are interactive in no way, shape, or form. The extremes of that model would present the example of detachment with severity.

For example, if a Deaf individual was murdering a Hearing person in front of you when you were on the job, you, as the interpreter, would interpret for the murderer as he stabs his victim. You could not intervene, acknowledge the affect it had on you, or acknowledge the severity of the action at hand. You would simply interpret for the murder, then walk away. Cheery scenario, I know, yet it does emphasize the cosmic detachment supported by this model when advocated by extremists. We all could explain the merits of this level of impartiality back in the day, although many of us felt the tug of elements not allotted for in this theory. This was one of those times.

My student was not doing well. I am more rigid about boundaries in my 40's than I was in my 20's, but even then, I knew a challenging judgment call had to be made. I obviously had to maintain a formal interpreter relationship with the student, but I decided if the kid wanted to vent after an event, once the work day was over and everyone was officially off duty, I would allow the venting. Week after week the student spouted frustrations, and I listened. Then one day, the student looked at me and said, "Sam, I am alive today because of you." That statement said the listening was worth it. Yeah, some people might say "That's not your job", "A counselor would be better", "You are just there to interpret", and normally I would agree, but all that kid needed was for someone to stop and let a silent voice be heard, period. It was a judgment call, and it worked. I also knew if amid the listening I saw there was something serious forming under the surface, then I could intervene in an appropriate manner. Some of you may want to burn me at the stake for letting that kid vent. I was looking at the bigger picture, and in retrospect, I have no regrets. Do I recommend you do that regularly? No. Have I done that many times in my career? No. Was it worth it that time? Yes. I abided by the Code of Ethics, I didn't break school rules, but I did push my big toe past my present day version of SIBS. Again, no regrets.

– Facebooking... What's the Harm? –

Every so often I run into an interpreter that passes off their personal information to their clients. Suddenly, clients become Facebook buddies, fellow Tweeters, Pinterest pals, and somehow this familiarity feels like a safe level of relationship to maintain. Not so much.

Every time a client has access to your personal information, they have access to YOU and that can be problematic. Being Facebook friends may seem innocent, I mean, isn't everybody? But when you write about your personal feelings, your activities that day, your vacations, etc., you are opening the door for a client to enter your mind and your emotions on an intimate level which can be problematic. I know, there are times interpreters end up offering their info, and it doesn't cause a problem. I know there are times when interpreters offer their info and they end up married to the man of their dreams. OK, "bigger picture". I get it.

However, on the whole, I think it's wise to keep social networking in check.

Here are some suggestions: If you use Facebook, have a professional Facebook page in addition to your personal one. This tends to be a safer way to keep relationships compartmentalized. On your professional Facebook page, avoid adding "likes" for personal preferences, rather keep them focused on professional interests. Avoid adding too much personal information, but definitely list career related information. Keep your verbiage professional. Consider it an opportunity to advertise your services, gather support for your Deaf Community interests, and educate viewers about interpreting.

For your personal Facebook page, use a version of your name which makes searching for you, and finding you, a bit more complicated so you can pick and choose who has access to that page. There you can handle your Facebook page in a far more personal and intimate manner. If you are careful you can keep your relationships with the community positive, interactive, but still private.

Socializing, social networking, and sharing personal information seem like conflicts we need to address, but what do you do when faced with the simple basic challenge of consumers asking for your phone number? Let's assume your "perfect man" is not the one asking you for a number, if he is, whip out that ball point and keep that fish from getting away, you have my permission. However, if he is not the Deaf version of Daniel Sunjata, Matt Bomer, or Channing Tatum (excuse the straight girl talk), and the person asking is an ordinary client, we arrive at the question, "Do you pass out your number?" This is one of the best reasons to keep a business card. If someone asks you for your information, you can hand them a business card and say, "You can reach me at this number." It works great. What if you need to contact someone at an assignment? I always suggest wisdom. Avoid it whenever possible, but if you can't (e.g.: if you have to contact the consumer when arriving on site for them to let you in a locked building) and you have a client who seems like they could be a problem, have your agency text them from the company cell phone, use a text to email system, or find an app that blocks your number. If you feel handing out your number will pose a problem, don't. You have to take care of yourself, which in the end protects your clients and your agencies.

– Touchy Feely Are We? –

What do you do when you are interpreting for a touchy feely person? How do you handle being a touchy feely person? The fact is, you should never touch a consumer. It protects you from accusations or implications, and it's physically safer. If you need to get their attention, try to find another way to do it rather than using touch. Touch is rather intimate. However, if the seating arrangement, the physical limitations of your consumer, or something of that nature requires you to touch your consumer, keep all touching in a neutral spot. Obviously, I don't need to say that interpreting for Deaf/Blind individuals is quite different. In general though, I suggest a "hands off policy" for safety and personal security.

What do you do if your consumer is touchy feely? It has happened to me. I have been with a consumer whom I am convinced wanted a little more than just interpreting services. When that happens, I keep a greater distance. I opt for the, "Oh, excuse me while I cough" option if they come toward me, and the, "I need to use the bathroom" excuse is quite handy when necessary. It's a good idea if you are concerned about your consumer, find yourself needing to make a phone call to kill time, or do whatever you can to keep a distance between you and that consumer which breeds concern.

– Team Lines –

We have discussed lines in the sand with your consumers, but what about with your teams? Sometimes lines in the sand can be very helpful. I have worked with all types of team interpreters, and although some have been an absolute dream come true, others have made me contemplate revisiting my childhood dream of becoming a trainer at Sea World. There have been a few times that team boundaries inadvertently became a life saving device. I have run across a few terps who have proven if they have any personal connection with you, they will mislay the necessary personal distance needed to work with you in a suitable manner. Whenever possible, when entering an assignment, I try to get to know just a little about my team. A little question like, "Are you from around here?" can break the ice enough to allow for a quick evaluation of the individual, and then hopefully, from that association, a more effective team rapport can ensue. Sometimes, it doesn't work out quite so smoothly.

Here's an example. One time I was working with an individual. Let's call her Martha. Martha had issues. She was a reasonable interpreter; her skills weren't a huge concern. What clearly became a problem was her ability to manage boundaries on a job. Martha and I sat down for lunch one day. We chose to eat together. We had only been on assignments together a few times, and it looked like more were on the horizon. As we sat down, she launched into the story of her own sexual abuse (we were on a political assignment so I have no idea how on earth that happened), and in three minutes I knew things about her which were straight out of a Lifetime movie. I felt like asking, "Could we table this discussion until I know if you are married and have kids?" I avidly worked at eating my not-so-exciting cold-cut sandwich as she regaled me with her horrific tales. Alright, she needed to talk, and I wanted to be supportive, but it became clear that support from a semi-stranger was not what she needed nor wanted. I didn't exactly know what she needed; I know I needed to finish that sandwich and hightail it to the safety of the bathroom as fast as my stubby Greek legs could carry me. Needless to say, she had a problem with boundaries. In Martha's case, I had to make sure when we were on assignments, I always carried food with me. It was a pre-smartphone time in history so an Angry Birds fix wasn't a viable solution, but I could keep myself distracted on breaks through old fashioned methods like eating or reading. Knowing boundaries were always going to be crossed, and not in minor ways, I opted to "be busy" for future lunches. It worked out well, and it kept a balanced relationship in place for the future.

I have had some wonderful experiences with teams, and some terrifying ones that nearly drove me to alcohol. Check out my chapter on team interpreting and you can see why boundaries become even more necessary in some cases.

Overall keep in mind, drawing a line in the sand is a very important decision for interpreters to make. It's definitely a very personal decision and one that needs to be made with care. I don't believe anyone can assert a definitive prerequisite for all Deaf, Hearing, or interpreter interaction. Like doctors and nurses, we all have our own styles and methodology. In the end, we do need to be able to do our jobs effectively, while maintaining balanced relationships with our consumers and fellow interpreters, that is, unless he or she is the future love of your life. Remember though, try to formulate your viewpoints prior to arriving at your personal crossroads. You will then be packing the ammo needed to set the standards which are right for you.

TERZIS' TIPS!

GOING "OLD SCHOOL" CAN SAVE THE DAY

Some of us are old enough to remember going to assignments via a map or written directions. GPS? When I started interpreting, they hadn't yet conceived of a pager, much less a basic cell phone. A Garmin or a smartphone with a built in GPS was a tiny bit out of reach. The only devices with GPS at that time were government missiles (I would assume) and the government wasn't concerned with loaning us the GPS systems so we could make it to freelance assignments on time. Older terps, do you remember having to stop to find a pay phone because you couldn't find your assignment? Oh yeah. You newbies have it good! Here's the deal though, interpreters today *DEPEND* on technology, which can get them into trouble! Sometimes, an old school mindset will save the day!

Print your directions! If you are in a downtown area with large buildings, or if you are in an extremely rural area, your GPS might not work. Something might happen to your GPS like your battery dying, a brake inspired dashboard impact, or an unexpected soda bath. If that happens, suddenly, no directions, and no on time arrival at the assignment happens too. What are you going to do if tragedy strikes your technology? If you have directions to your freelance assignments printed and in hand, you can find your way to the designated location, technology crisis or not. I can't tell you the number of times we have received calls in our office because of GPS failures. It became such a problem that we started hounding our interpreters to print the provided directions and when they did so, lo and behold the GPS calls stopped coming. Remember people, technology can be your friend, and your enemy. Use it wisely, but always be prepared for it not to work.

WORKING IN "TEAMS"

This chapter could get really long! I have had some interesting experiences working with team interpreters. Some experiences have been fabulous! Some experiences have mauled my emotional state... for life. Being a team interpreter is an important business, and I don't claim to have been a perfect team member. I have had good days and bad days like the rest of you, but one thing is certain, it's better to be a *GREAT* team interpreter. Let's talk about how you can achieve this.

– Do Your Job –

The title of this section should make you think, "This can't be good." It's not. Sadly, many team interpreters forget a few very important facts: they are interpreting, and they are a part of someone's "team". I know, the name should be a dead give-away, but it must not be! Let's start with *actually assisting* the person with whom you are assigned to work.

Thank God I am running a company now that the great invention of the easily accessible smartphone has entered the interpreting world. My team interpreters have enough of a healthy fear of working with me that they don't try to sit eternally on their smartphones and ignore assisting me when I am in the hot seat. I have a little hearing loss due to an ear injury as a child and that hearing loss will sometimes cause me to miss a word. It's nice when I have a "back-up" to feed me that elusive term. I like having a team. However, I don't like teams that ignore me because they are talking with their friends, texting, or these days checking their smartphones for the latest Facebook status of a friend.

A team interpreter should be attentive to their team, offer signs when they are signaled, get their team water if he/she is coughing, write feedback down if requested, and even look-up technical jargon or information on the internet via *their smartphones* if the interpreter is struggling with a complicated word or concept. The team interpreter should *HELP*. He/she should live up to the name *"TEAM"*. I have been dumbfounded hearing horror stories about team interpreters. Stories like one interpreter saying to her team, "Well, that isn't my job" when the interpreter requested water, or another story of a team member on a stage job refusing to get help for the struggling terp on duty. I think that attitude is appalling. A *team* Interpreter, by its very nature, should be someone working alongside and in tandem with another interpreter. That person's time out of the hot seat is not nap time, surf time, flirt time, or whatever. It's still work time. Please don't misunderstand. Most of us are women. Potty breaks are necessary, and if you have a situation where an off duty team member needs to take a potty break, and it can be done without incredible distraction or degradation to an assignment, go tee-tee. It's all good. Not returning because you are in the middle of a 45 minute chat with a hot guy in the hallway, not so good. If you are a team interpreter, try and be on the job and available at all times, and please be willing to serve your team with more than just a missed word. Attentiveness and service really do matter.

– Feeding Your Team –

We all have different methods of how or when we like to be fed. Again, I have heard horror stories, and interacted with interpreters myself who are "anti-team," interpreters who, with well-rehearsed snippiness say, "Don't feed me, I am fine." Ok, I won't. If an interpreter with her undies in a wad spouts off a remark like that, I open up a book and read. If the consumer asks me why I am not helping my team interpreter, I say, "She instructed me not to assist her." I have seen a consumer or two get angry, knowing the person on the job needed assistance, but I figure they can duke it out. I can't force someone to accept my assistance. I can offer. They can refuse. I can choose not to work with that individual in the future. I prefer working with happy people.

Now, sometimes people don't feed well. I made a mistake once a few years ago. It's wasn't a traumatic event, but I am a perfectionist of sorts and I was disappointed in the Sam faux pas. I was working on no sleep for an extended period of time and it showed. At one point my team was voicing and left a gap while she was formulating her thoughts. She's a CODA and a great voice interpreter. I was pondering what was being said while in my sleepless stupor, and I let something slip as a feed, knowing she was probably just working through the info in her head. The gloss won no awards, and I threw my poor team interpreter momentarily. Bad Sam. I learned something that day. SLEEP! It's very important. Told you I was human. For some though, it's not a bad day, it's a bad methodology which drives their teaming skills. Let's delve into some of the issues surrounding the methods team interpreters choose to feed their partners on a job.

– Asking for a Feed –

It's a good idea to take a moment before an assignment and decide how you will ask for a feed. For example, if sitting side-by-side, will you touch the person's leg? Will you elbow the person? Will you lean and speak into his/her ear? If face to face, will you just look at your team using that all important eye contact? Find a method that works for you. One time, I forgot to discuss this with a team interpreter, and I ended up getting groped on assignment (hopefully unintentionally). Assignments are not really the time for groping. Let's say, pre-planning is much safer.

– Feeding Amounts –

We all have different feeding preferences. Some people like it when they are fed full sentences. I prefer individual words. Years ago, I had an interpreter feed me from an audience, and she would go back 3 sentences and re-sign everything which had just been signed in order to provide for me the one word I couldn't hear. That wasn't too helpful. The distance, the lighting, the crowd noises, were not bad enough, now you are going to confuse me with restated info. STOP! Even when I asked her to feed me just a few words, she refused. Nope, that was not helpful at all. I strongly encourage you to find out how much information your team wants you to feed in advance, and feed that amount only.

– Signed Language or System –

Do you feed in ASL or PSE/Contact? Each interpreter has their individual preferences. Personally, I like being fed in PSE. I will change the PSE to ASL in my head, but it's easier for me to manage where it's going when I see it as it was originally spoken. When my teams feed me with a complicated ASL structure defined as they would structure something themselves, I end up having to awkwardly copy their facial expressions and movements. It never comes off as successful as when the speaker originally presented the info. We all formulate sentences differently in ASL. One of my majors in college was Art, which means I tend to structure ASL like a photo. My team interpreter might be more regulated by linear ASL elements. Those differences might force me into a re-interpretation of the fed translation so that the final product fits my personal style of interpreting. In the end, when someone feeds me using ASL, I ponder not only what they said, but how they said it. My brain has enough to do with all the extra mumbo jumbo required for any interpreting assignment, in addition to the insanity lurking in the complicated brain of a female. Who needs more to ponder? I prefer skipping the middle steps, and have my team feed me in PSE thereby allowing me to generate the ASL gloss. Mind you, that is only *my* preference. You have to decide what works best for you.

– Feed Fully or Moderately –

I am personally not a fan of people feeding me with vigor. I prefer less movement, less drama, more clarity. Why? I am listening for what I missed, watching the feed for specifics, reformulating the presented signs into my version of the interpretation, and keeping up with what is being said, all while I am getting my feed. Adding incredible amounts of facial expression, movement, body shifting, and signed drama gives me more to think about, and to quote a well-known adage, in this case, "less is more". Let's not disregard the distraction; when a team interpreter launches into a dramatically expressed feed for an interpretation, especially in tight quarters, the Deaf automatically turn and look at the team interpreter for the missing information. They are Deaf! They are always scoping out their environment, and the severe hand flapping happening just out of their eye-shot is too much of a curiosity to ignore. Honestly, I think it causes more distraction than help. I personally think it's better to feed clearly without extensive movement or drama. Keep it mellow. Your teams will thank you.

– Feeding with Fingerspelling –

I can't express enough how annoying it is to get a sentence or two fed via rapid and lazy fingerspelling when you are relying on a team interpreter. I have had team interpreters try and "show their stuff" by fingerspelling hastily and slothfully so they look "Deaf" and "cool". Well, it's lovely that your "cool factor" has been upped a notch in your mind, but I need the info, so slow down and be clear, because I have 10 things in my head besides your lazy fingerspelling issues! (And all the annoyed interpreters say, "Amen!") I mean, where did the misconception begin that "fast fingerspelling" makes you "cool"? Is speed the prerequisite for "cool" in this business? If you are my team, I need you to be clear... period.

Limit your fingerspelling when possible. Sometimes a word will find its salvation in a sign which is clearly mouthed, no fingerspelling necessary. An example: "Athens" and "Iran" are the same sign. If the speaker is talking about that part of the world, and you missed the name of the location, you can sign the "name sign" and mouth ATHENS to make sure the interpreter knows which locale was being discussed. It's quicker, easier, and clearer than spelling A-T-H-E-N-S. Another example is a book title, one which has equivalent signs, being announced to a class by an instructor. If the team spells the entire title, it could take extra time, and be difficult to understand. However, if the team signs, "The Six Wives of Henry VIII," keeping fingerspelling limited to only proper names, it becomes easy to read. True, there are times when fingerspelling is the only option. For example, what about the movie *Armageddon*? Fingerspell that one I guess. Then again you could go with Seeing Essential English (SEE 1) and opt for something along the lines of ARM+A+GET+ON. Haha! Just kidding! Don't do that! I digress. What I am saying is sign what you can and spell as little as possible. It makes everything go more smoothly.

– Be Helpful –

I know it's hard to believe, but Team interpreters should actually strive to be helpful. One time I was interpreting for a famous speaker on stage. In spite of all my efforts to have the right sound equipment available, the techies left me without any sound. I was challenged to say the least. I found myself very reliant on my team. To add to the challenge, apparently the lady directly across from me in this 17,000 person arena was either a big fan, or she had just had a psychotic break. She screamed at the top of her lungs for as long as one can imagine. I kept envisioning the many ways I could shut her up. Sling shot... check. BB gun... check. A football thrown from a Tennessee Titan... check, and she kept screaming. Now, had I not had a deficient team that day, things could have improved quickly; however, she was a team interpreter of little intrinsic value, and so the assignment went downhill fast.

How could she have supported me? First option, *SHUT THE WOMAN UP!* Silly me, it seemed so logical. Apparently, it wasn't to her. She could have gone to an usher and had the woman's perpetual fandom placed under control. No such luck. What she did, which was so helpful (please note the sarcasm in that statement), was scream, "Sam, get off the stage, I understand black people better than you do. I can do better!" Are you kidding me? Let's walk through the situation: a) I couldn't hear because I didn't have a monitor and the looney across from me was trying to drive me to self-harm, b) yes, the speaker was black and I am Greek-ish, but his marginally different vocalization patterns were not really as much of a difficulty as, work with me here, the *CRAZY SCREAMING WOMAN* right in front of me, and c) it would have gone slightly more smoothly if, again, work with me here, *SHE WOULD HAVE FED ME!* Oh yeah. That was a fun assignment. I have forgotten many things in my career but that day was far too much of a mental keeper to lose. She opted not to be helpful, she wanted more stage time, and she clearly didn't win any team interpreter awards that day. I felt pretty successful though, I didn't cause her physical harm when it was over. It's the little "wins" we accomplish every day that help keep us positive.

I had another incident where I was working with a CODA. He had a less than favorable reputation. I tried to stay out of the gossip, but it didn't take me long to figure out why he remained the center of city wide chatter among interpreters!

Right before this assignment began, I was nearly killed in a car accident having been hit by a drunk driver who had run a red light. Of course, after a severe accident, I found myself surviving by the hands of medical clinicians who were providing physical therapy and much needed pain medications. The pain medication I was taking caused extreme bouts of nausea. Apparently, the meds had irritated the lining of my stomach, and as a result I was throwing up toilet bowls full of blood. (TMI?) It was awful. I wasn't sure which was worse, the pain, or the nausea. I was single and I had to pay the bills, so agony or no agony, I mustered up a smile, packed my body with meds, and I went to work every day. If you have been single in the working world, it's likely you understand; health is a luxury, and the need to get the rent paid and food on the table wins over comfort, convenience, or preference sometimes.

I was excited about the assignment. Most educational assignments of this type hold a special place in my heart. The material was complicated, and the experience I knew would be challenging, yet I knew also it would have a positive impact on my growth as an interpreter. What I didn't realize was that my team interpreter was of the devil! In only days, he started trying to sabotage my rapport with the consumers. How? There are far too many ways to define here. He was definitely on a mission. One quick example: I would voice for my consumer, and he would suddenly voice on top of me. Was he correcting what I was saying? Nope. He would use the exact same words I was using, in the exact same order, but the action served its purpose. It was his attempt to demean me on the job. I was a twenty-something interpreter; I admit, I didn't know how to respond. He used a variety of similar methods to breed distrust and negative attention towards me, and his scheme worked. His many approaches to Sam degradation strained my relationship with the Deaf consumer and raised an eyebrow or two from the Hearing consumers. The Deaf consumer was also a friend, and our relationship never recovered from what he did. He won. Mission accomplished.

He attacked me with an agenda which I never understood. I didn't even know him well prior to the assignment. One source of his forceful abduction of all respect for me may have been to turn attention from his own issues. For example, he would fall asleep in class, then snore. I don't mean a cute wheezing type of snore, I mean a bear like, growling sort of snore which would, in some cases, cause the instructor to have to shout over his vocalizations. That happened weekly, and in what was a likely attempt to be supportive of the Deaf consumer, the action was ignored by the professors and students. His personal attempts at humiliation and clearly defined malfeasance were topped only by his "kindness" towards me. (More sarcasm for you zinger lovers.) One of my favorite memories of working with him was when I would get nauseated on the job. On occasion, I would get violently ill from the medicine I had been given, and I would quickly develop the need to have one of those colorful toilet bowl experiences. The consumers never knew how sick I had been. I was pretty good at managing the appearance of a functioning interpreter in front of them. When I got out of the hot seat though, it could get rough, and I could sometimes create a scene in the bathroom which looked more like a CSI episode, than the conduction of my then daily routine. One day, in particular, I was working with this Team interpreter, and when his twenty minutes were up, realizing I was building towards a moment of colorful bathroom drama, I asked him to continue interpreting for an additional five minutes so I could relinquish my lunch (and likely the lining of my stomach). He looked at me, knowing I was ill, and said, "No. It's your turn. Do your job." I was tempted just to throw-up on him at that point, which I could have done with ease, but I decided to refrain, not for his sake, but for that of the consumers. I took my turn to interpret. I was so sick, and combatting the churning in my stomach was a battle I never want to relive. I barely made it through. I had to calm myself and focus intensely on what needed to be signed, trying to pay no attention to the sounds and cramps coming from my midsection. When time for "the switch" arrived, I hightailed it to the bathroom, and anointed the commode once again. "Thanks dude! I appreciate the support!" That was helpful. (Note my sarcasm here). I must admit despondently, he actually enjoyed hurting me. His heart made me sad for him. I think as brothers & sisters in the field, we should support each other and not find reasons to wound each other.

– Drop Negative Agendas –

Sometimes interpreters have specific agendas, and they bring those agendas to their assignments. I have seen a wide variety of agendas, some more damaging than others. It goes without saying that critical agendas and the desire to promote oneself while tearing others down, should be removed from the to-do list while on assignment. One of my interns left our company to go to D.C. for a while. She wasn't a perfect interpreter (are any of us?), but she had a lot of natural talent and she was definitely skilled. She had been trained in a four year program in the Mid-West. She arrived in D.C. with passion and enthusiasm. I was concerned at how a small town girl would handle a big, *big* city, but she was ready to face whatever came, and I respected her passion and determination. She landed an internship at a reputable company with, what sounded like, a skilled mentor. That was the beginning of what nearly became the end of her career. I was told that her mentor turned negative criticism into a daily tic mark on her personal agenda. This intern knew her faults before she left, but clearly that mentor showed up with a plan to prove her own superiority by degrading her mentee. A comment about a different sign choice would be expelled from her lips in the form of a barrading barrage of negativity about the intern's skill set. Was that necessary? The girl was her team. The looks, the comments, the attacks lessened her effectiveness, and as her psyche was injured, her confidence and skills followed suit leaving a broken and aggrieved young woman. The intern left her assignments daily in tears, defeated and alone. In a short time she was ready to leave the field, and why? Because a seasoned interpreter showed up with an agenda instead of a heart. I am sure that interpreter could justify her reasoning with statements referring to the merits of criticism as "learning about the real world," or "handling the toughest of interpreters and clientele," but what she did was wound and destroy an underling because of her own personal negative agenda. It wasn't necessary, and it wasn't right.

Does this sound like you? Please stop and consider this: is the legacy you want to leave in the minds and the souls of people you work with, a legacy of pain? Does wounding others help you? I believe every criticism from a team or mentor doesn't just leave a blemish on the heart of the interpreter receiving the criticism; it leaves a mutation on the soul of the person giving it.

What other negative agendas do interpreters have outside of criticism? One of my personal favorites has been, "Let's not interpret today." Yeah, that one really happened. This is a good story, so no coffee or bathroom breaks for the duration.

I was called to interpret a college class. It was a three hour class so two interpreters were placed on the assignment. The student wasn't motivated. He was a nice kid, but college was more of "something to do" rather than a goal. My team on that job used that apathy for her own agenda one day encouraging him *NOT* to pay attention or participate in class. Apparently some conversation ensued prior to my arrival which illuminated the goals for the day, "No work. Play only." I apparently didn't get the RID memo which defined that additional set of changes to the old Code of Ethics, changes which must have stated that our moods or preferences should guide the extent of our participation in a class. Oops. I should read my mail more carefully. We sat down and she said, "We decided not to work today, so you don't need to interpret." I was so confused. Are you kidding? What interpreter would do that? I was in an ethical dilemma on so many levels, and I had to decide what to do. I looked at the clock when the class started, I waited my usual 20 minutes, and I started interpreting. She said, "He doesn't care what you are saying, why are you interpreting?" (Uh, I don't know. It's my job?) When my twenty minutes were over, I stopped interpreting, and they kept talking. When twenty minutes had passed, I started to interpret again, and so on. At one point she grabbed my arms and held them down saying, "He doesn't care. Rest!" She held my arms down? Who does that? Clearly, her agenda was *NOT* to interpret. It goes without saying that her agenda should have been left at the door. Well, it probably should have been left in bed before her feet hit the floor that morning. She impacted that student's education, she upset and distracted the instructor, she distracted the class, she caused me distress, and to top it off, she landed in this book. It's a good example of the damage a negative agenda can do. It just didn't need to happen. Table the unhealthy agendas. Focus on doing a great job, and if you ever choose an agenda, keep it an un-invasive and positive one.

– Enjoy Yourself –

There is no rule about not enjoying working with your team. Undoubtedly, I want my team members to be professional (and not hold my arms down when I interpret), but the best teaming experiences I have had were when my teams would laugh with me, act friendly, supportive, and fun. I don't believe you should show up on your job with an attitude. We have talked about arrogance, and hopefully you see how that is not ideal, but showing up without a smile and a friendly demeanor can, in actuality, negatively influence the effectiveness of a team relationship.

Time for another story. Not a big one, just a little example. Years ago, I worked with an interpreter from a local agency. I was on staff at a college at the time, and she was hired for teaming in a particular class. She showed up with a pessimistic demeanor. She wasn't "out to get me", she wasn't arrogant, well maybe a little, but primarily she just looked like acknowledging my presence was incredibly low on her priority list. When I tried to speak to her, she barely answered me back. When I discussed our teaming plan, she sometimes ignored me. The coldness she expressed affected our effectiveness as a team, it impacted the student, it left a heaviness in the room, and in the end, it did far more damage than she realized. Had she shown up with a smile, everything about the class would have gone better.

Your presence makes a difference for your team. Being professional doesn't include frowning, showing extreme distance or control. Being a team, by its very nature, means working together, supporting each other, and creating an effective environment for the other interpreter and the consumer. When you walk on to your next job, stop and consider *HOW* you walk on to your next job. It might change the legacy you leave, as well as create the perfect environment for everyone to succeed.

TERZIS' TIPS!

FEELING TRAPPED?

Sometimes you feel trapped on a job. Sometimes the feeling is caused by the job itself or it might be from the people with whom you work. (They probably haven't read this book yet; you could buy them a copy!) But no matter what, remember that speaking and thinking positively can improve a situation. Your words have power. If you complain about your situation, if you regularly make comments about how frustrated you are, even if you just sit around pondering the negative aspects of your situation, you are definitely empowering negative things to happen. Here's a quick tip. When things start "going south", start speaking positively. If the problem is your team interpreter's negativity, instead of thinking, "Her complaining is driving me crazy," try saying something like, "I look forward to the delightful variation from her present state of pessimism to her future expressions of joy." Instead of saying, "I hate my boss," try saying something like, "I am feeling challenged by my boss, but change is coming!" If your consumer is an irritable jerk, instead of thinking, "Please don't show today. Please don't show today", try thinking something like, "I look forward to being a professional and a light in his otherwise dark world." A little attitude shift from you can make a radical difference in the people around you. It might take a while, or you might see a change in them the first day, but when you feel trapped, you likely have more power than you realize. Use it!

FEELING A LITTLE HOLEY?

Interpreters, sadly, betray each other. We have sort of inherited an "every man for himself" attitude. I think as the field developed, we began to get protective of our jobs and our skills. Our insecurities caused us to worry that others would "get ahead" and we would not be wanted or respected. Those fears have ruled us. I remember one day at one of our workshops, an interpreter said to me, "Thank you for actually *sharing* what you learned, and letting us use your experiences to get better. So many interpreters don't want to share what they know." Sadly, she was right. Many do not want to let people in on their secrets, the secret of their successes, and definitely not their failures. One of the reasons I am writing this book and teaching my workshops is to do just that. I believe I only get one shot at this life, and I want to leave the interpreting world better than when I found it. Maybe my honesty can help make that happen? I hope it does. However, most interpreters don't have that perspective. So how do interpreters often shield themselves and their careers? They choose betrayal and gossip.

– Stabbing Your Agencies –

How many stories have I heard of betrayal in the interpreting world? Since I run an agency, let's talk about betraying your agencies. If you accept a job through a particular agency, do not work that job outside the agency. That's a basic ethical standard. We had one situation where two interpreters went to an assignment. We suddenly noticed that one member of the team was not taking jobs from us. Eventually we discovered the organization had convinced one of the interpreters to work directly for them without working through us as her agency. I am sure she had a litany of reasons why it was "the right decision" for her. She doesn't realize it, but her actions were a form of betrayal. Her actions shattered a standard held by individuals in the industry all over our nation. What should she have done? She should have either stated to the people making the request that she had a responsibility to our organization as the original assignment was booked through us, or she could have asked for our endorsement in accepting it. Neither of those things happened. She took the job, and backed away from our company, causing us an enormous amount of strain personally and professionally.

It then happened again! Suddenly, we noticed that we were not receiving calls from a particular organization which had been regularly sending us work.

Later, they contacted us for an interpreter. The individual making the request said, "Our sub _[name deleted]_ is not available. Can you all fill this job?" The sub was our interpreter! OXYGEN! We were incredibly disappointed in the choices that interpreter made. She broke our trust that first day, then intentionally or unintentionally, time and time again on future days. I am sure even today she believes her choices were validated in some way, but by American interpreting standards, she has not won any integrity awards.

Betraying your agency can also come in the form of breaking the rules. We have specific guidelines for our interpreters. We had one young interpreter who was very gifted, but was facing some personal problems. Her reaction to these off job issues was to rebel, and since she couldn't confront the problem directly where it was initiated, she brought those feelings of rebellion and anger to the job. Goody. We found out that she started ignoring the requests of her lead interpreter. She began chatting with the clients at conferences during a presentation. Then she started grumbling about "yours truly" when I wasn't present. I have the maturity to know the reason for her actions had nothing to do with me directly; she was mentally trying to work through her personal issues and needed an outlet for her frustrations. What she did, though, was inadvertently attack our company. I don't believe it was her initial intent; she was just venting emotions which had been building in her personal pressure cooker for years. In the end, the source of that frustration was not where she directed her scowls and bitterness; our agency ended up with a temporary target on our back. It wasn't right, and it wasn't fair. She may or may not ever acknowledge what had transpired. Loyalty carries a great deal of significance, even to agencies. Before you make choices which can hurt your personal or professional relationships, before you make choices which can be misdirected, stop and consider whether your planned actions are worth what seems to be the immediate benefit.

Agency betrayal can also come in the form of gossip. Interpreters love gossip. Every single one of us has given into it at some point on some miniscule level. Some interpreters get frustrated with their agencies, and their response is to publicly complain about them.

We all get frustrated with our jobs. However, it's important to remember that your job is your livelihood, and your method of handling your job can and does influence people's perspective of your integrity. We sometimes feel immune to other's perceptions, but we are not. I have seen it happen. An interpreter becomes angry at an agency for any of a variety of reasons. It's possible the agency sent him/her to a job which is obviously different than what was originally conveyed. It's possible that checks are delayed, or agency preferences don't match those of the interpreters. It's possible the standards of the agency for attire, wait times, or team choices seem questionable to that interpreter. The unsatisfied interpreter's response: defame the agency. What's the benefit? It's true some agencies make bad choices. Some have standards which are questionable. Some have a staff which resembles Hitler's regime, far more than the loving nature of Mr. Roger's Neighborhood. Many agencies have incredibly good intentions, and some agencies do not. It's easy to find agencies riddled with imperfections, and hopefully others have just a few. However, stop and think, when is any job perfect? I am definitely not saying interpreters should lie, or falsely shed words of approval and glee about an assignment or characteristics of an agency when clearly there is something which needs to be altered; however an interpreter also doesn't need to become the source of gossip and contention. If something negative arises, contact your agency. Discuss the situation. Work it out, but don't publicly and verbally condemn it.

Your integrity is important. Your agency may be a quality organization, or might be a very frustrating place to work, but remember, whatever your agency is like, whatever your school is like, whatever your company is like, or whatever your religious institution is like, be sure to handle your job with professionalism, with a smile, and yes, with integrity.

– Stabbing Interpreters –

Have you ever worked with interpreters and felt like you were back in Jr. High? Think about it, in Jr. High young teens merged into cliques, they gossiped about each other, their emotions were erratic, they were never at fault, and they were almost always critical. It sounds exactly like the interpreting world doesn't it? (¾ of you want to squeeze the dickens out of me right now for that statement, and a ¼ of you I am sure are plotting my demise.) If you don't think so, you either a) work in a city to which I need to move (so be sure to send me the address), b) you have had an optimal career of which many are likely jealous, or c) you might be a tiny bit more involved in the drama than you realize. The fact is that the characteristics which nearly drove us to insanity in our youth are the very ones which I have seen surface among many of our fellow interpreters. Before you call for that hit man and start rattling off my address, let me tell you that I have talked to literally hundreds and hundreds of interpreters in America who agree with what I just said. Please don't attack me; put the bashing remark you just formulated for your Facebook page on hold, and listen to what I have been told so many interpreters are dying for someone to say.

I dream of interpreters supporting each other, encouraging each other, without all the added rubbish. Have you been a victim of this behavior? Have you worked with a group of interpreters who seemed to be "BFFs," who left you sitting by yourself, clearly unwelcomed? Have you been the target of "what I know about her..." stories? Have you had the joy of working with critical interpreters, gossiping interpreters, hateful interpreters, or condescending interpreters? Have interpreters ever driven you to tears? Have you ever felt like Caesar with knives sticking out of your back? I know I have.

Although I have been the center of more than one dramatic mauling (lucky me), there is one scenario which definitely stands out in my mind. I was working with a group of new and experienced interpreters who now become the highlight of this personal chronicle. Our initial characters in the story were once dear friends of mine. Let's call them Stella and Helen. (Cue novella music.) Stella was having trouble in her marriage and was looking for something or someone to blame. Helen was feeling torn emotionally after a divorce. Stella and Helen became buddies in the midst of their personal traumas. What did they have in common outside of marital challenges? A love for sign language, and me. (Increase dramatic novella music.) Their pent up frustration, pent up anger, and pent up irritation in their personal lives needed an outlet, and I was conveniently located nearby. *FUN!* Everything I did, or had done years prior, was scrutinized, manipulated, and then twisted to somehow become the reason for a personal attack. The result? A "Burn Sam in Effigy" party. They gathered other interpreters into the "Attack Sam Mob", and before long I was sitting on the sidelines bandaging my wounds, and wondering what the heck I had done to deserve all of the "love" and "attention" bestowed on me from the very people I had worked alongside, educated, inspired, and loved. It was crazy. It was destructive. It was an official "interpreter stabbing". They actually made it their mission for a time to take me down. Who would do that? Well, obviously, they would. Sadly, they aren't the only ones.

Attacks like that leave scars on those wielding the knife, just as they do on the person on the receiving end of the attack. I saw the stains on their lives and in their careers. I am sure they convinced themselves that they were justified in their actions, but so does the KKK. What did they accomplish? Was it truly for the greater good? Do they wake-up every day now feeling peace because they nearly destroyed my life? It never works like that. The attackers become the wounded. They feel empty inside, and then that emptiness fuels future attacks. It's an ongoing cycle which is difficult to break, and I see it all across the country.

Radical assaults on another person should never be encouraged or justified. Before you find someone to maul, ponder this: would you want to be the victim in that scenario? I think we should always fall back on love and support of our fellow interpreters. We should be cheerleaders for each other. We should be a sounding board, a helping hand, a shoulder to cry on, and a source of love and protection. We might all have different beliefs, we might dress differently, think differently, and even sign differently, but we are still a family. Too many interpreters have come to my office in tears because of the wounds created by others in the field. Too many people have stopped me at workshops thanking me profusely for words such as these. Too many people have left the field because of the attacks on their skills. Too many people have said, "I can't take it anymore." Far too many tears have been shed. It's time we make a change, and get back to the basics, professionalism, support, and love.

– When Band-Aids Don't Work –

If there is one radical truth about interpreters in America, it is that many are wounded people. Many have been beaten down, ostracized, debased, marginalized, targeted, and those actions have hurt. CODAs have been hurt, educational interpreters have been hurt, video interpreters have been hurt, and the freelancers have been hurt. Whether you are a pro or a newbie, you have likely incurred some form of a wound. I have seen far too many tears in my office and across America to ignore that pain. I want so much to see that change.

How can that change be made? I hate to do it. I am not a Beatles fan, but the fact is that they nailed this one. "All we need is love." After meeting people from coast to coast, I have found that what every individual in the world wants is *love*, and the way to start a wave of change in this field is by giving and receiving that simple four letter word. It comes in the form of encouragement on and off the job. It's shown through a hug on a bad day, or a willingness to listen to someone's frustrations. It's saying, "I trust you," or "I believe in you." It comes through when we show that someone matters even in the midst of our busy lives. We see it when we don't require perfection of each other, or when we can laugh together over our mistakes right before we strive to do better the next time. Love has power. Over time, it heals what a Band-Aid never could. Sadly, when we don't receive it (whether because it wasn't offered, we didn't recognize the offer, or we refuse to accept it) we feel the sting of that pain, and often we respond by becoming offended. From there the cycle of destructive behavior usually begins.

The offenses are important to address. When we have been stabbed in the back by interpreters or agencies, we can take-up an offense against them. We let their hurtful actions get under our skin. That festers into a desire to take revenge, or just to stay angry. It causes back-biting, gossip, rebellion, etc. Those emotions are like a splinter. If you leave them under your skin, they fester. So what's the answer if you have been the victim? Forgive. **Forgive.** *FORGIVE!* You can't take away the injustices and the wrongs done to you, but you can be determined to overcome them. The first way to do that is to love in spite of the target that is or was painted on your back, and the second way is to forgive. When an interpreter houses an offense, and uses it as an anchor for his/her personal stability, that offense also weighs down his/her peace, joy, happiness, and success. When an interpreter forgives and loves, the interpreter lets go of the weight and he/she is able to fly. The added benefit, is that the simple action of forgiveness has the power to heal wounds. Give it a try. If you forgive, you will likely make a change to your own life, and maybe in a few others as well. I have done it time and time again, and I have been able to move on from those places of hurt. Until someone puts down the weapons, the fighting will never end.

So what's the moral of this story? We need to change how we interact with each other, and with our employers. We need to think differently, act differently, and react differently. We need to love and be loved. If we do that, great things will happen in this field and in our own lives.

TERZIS' TIPS!

BAITING GRINS

I have found an incredible way to throw interpreters off, and cast vision in the process. What do I do? I am really, really, really nice to them, and I work vigilantly at making them smile. Let me give you an example. We had an interpreter in South who was sad. She was a very qualified interpreter, a respected interpreter, but she was an unhappy interpreter. I never saw her smile without concerted assistance. That challenge motivated me. I made it my mission to make her smile. I would joke with her. I would make sure my body language showed we were friends. I gave her lots of attention. Why? Because she needed to smile, and the only way I knew how to do it was try and bait her into lightening up and letting go. Most of the time, before we would leave an event, she would at least break a grin. If you know interpreters who are unhappy and are trying to mask their unhappiness with a variety of unhealthy coping mechanisms, try and make them smile. It's a great way to impact a life, and it's a fun challenge for you.

HOPING FOR NO COPING

Every person in America has unhealthy coping mechanisms. I think it's a requirement for being human. Sadly, those unhealthy coping mechanisms make being an interpreter not so much fun, because our fellow interpreters can be wrought full of icky coping skills. Coping skills come in a wide variety of formats. God help us when they get mixed with **PMS** or menopause! (And all the men say, AMEN!) It's true, sometimes life can stoke the already bright burning flame of our "out of balance" coping skills. The result? Everyone and everything suffers! The one spewing coping shrapnel can cause others to feel intimidated or afraid, it can cause offense or anger, it can lead to division, and it can lead to a less positive work environment. When coping mechanisms go unchecked and unmanaged, people are affected, work is affected, and no one sits around begging to work with that particular interpreter in the future. Let's review some common coping mechanisms which surface in the interpreting world, and see what we can do to manage those in our own lives.

Disclaimer: I do not claim to be a psychologist.
These are merely a lay person's observations.

– Denial –

Refusing to Accept Reality or Fact

Denial is incredibly tempting! You have heard it before. "I didn't do that." "I didn't say that." "I can do that." A thousand statements could be listed and you would still have more examples of how interpreters participate wholeheartedly in denial. Sometimes interpreters are in denial about their appearance. Sometimes they are in denial about their skills. Sometimes interpreters are in denial about their attitudes. Sometimes they are in denial about their actions. I guarantee you some people reading this book have been in denial thinking of all the *other* people who should read it, when so many of these faux pas have been their own. One thing is for sure, of any coping mechanism interpreters choose, denial is one of the favorites.

Skill Based Denial

I see this one ALL THE TIME! We had an interpreter apply with us who I was pretty sure appeared on our doorstep to scope out the competition. We accepted her into the fold with more than a little trepidation. Gate Communications has regular mini-workshops which encourages our interpreters to improve their skill set. One particular day, each interpreter stood up and provided an interpretation for the group. Each presentation was followed with a quickie evaluation. The interpreter in question finished her moment before the group, and after the first statement of critique, immediately started denying any error on her part. Everyone was a bit perplexed. We run the organization like a family. We are all very supportive of one another, so errors are seen as opportunities for improvement, not opportunities for condemnation. Alas, she was not a happy camper. In the end, she created a scene, drew an enormous amount of attention to herself, and for what? What did she gain? It didn't change the interpretation. Her denial didn't breed respect. It did however make people question her perspectives, and honestly, her maturity. If she had opted for a "denial free" response, no one would have thought any less of her.

The fact is we all make mistakes. What's the harm in admitting to them? She's definitely not the only one. Interpreters all over America pull these same dramatic exclamations at our national workshops. I think it's somehow assumed if a faux pas is vehemently denied, then suddenly it never existed. Now, I am not a temporal physicist. Honestly, addition and subtraction leave me baffled enough, but I don't believe that denial will alter the parameters of the Space-Time Continuum. At least, I have never seen it happen. Then again, maybe this *IS* an alternate universe and in another life I am really a size two! Nah, doubt it. Let's assume it doesn't work like that. What that indicates is that denial is a coping mechanism which doesn't leave the denier looking good, or the people watching the denial feeling warm and fuzzy inside. It leaves everyone feeling uneasy and uncomfortable. Next time you're tempted to deny something, just pause and think, "What's the harm in admitting to this?" Instead of, "I didn't do that" try, "Yeah, I was a bit bumfuzzled today." (It's an excuse to use the word bumfuzzled, which I personally think is a good thing.) Instead of saying, "I voiced that fine" when you know deep down you butchered what the poor Deaf person was trying to say, just say, "I didn't win a merit award for interpreting today." I promise, you will survive!

– Compensation –

A process of psychologically counterbalancing a perceived weaknesses by emphasizing one's strengths in other areas.

This one is far from uncommon. "Well, maybe I am not skilled at____, but I am good at _____." Sadly, a compensating interpreter believes that his/her lack of perfection in a particular area is something he/she needs to defend. Let me give you an example. I am not a Legal Interpreter. There is no hope I will be a phenomenal Legal Interpreter. Pursuing an SC:L to me is up there with a purposeless voluntary hysterectomy. I don't understand why anyone would want to do it! One day, I was pulled over in rural Tennessee. Apparently, the speed drops 10 MPH in a specific spot, and I didn't know it. I was in "podunk nowhere" at the time. The 55 MPH sign was located in a somewhat obscure area. In the end, it didn't matter, I was nailed. I went to the court date, and the judge wasn't a *judge*, he was someone else of power. He didn't wear a robe. No one said "Your Honor", and yet I sat there terrified. I was shaking when my name was called. Then my intimidation level got worse. Something fishy happened in the hearing with the Sherriff who had pulled me over. Honestly, unless I was imagining it, something illegal happened right there in the court room! Did I say anything? No. Wimpy (that would be me in this scenario) stood there petrified to state what seemed like an obvious act of corruption. I kept my mouth shut. I left there, and my first thought was, "I am definitely not called to Legal Interpreting." Geez. No brainer huh? 100,000 people in an audience, me on the stage, no problem, one guy sitting behind a big desk with a gavel, and I become eligible for a Depends commercial. Go figure! Am I a "bad interpreter" because I am not wired emotionally for Legal? No! I might be a bad Legal Interpreter. You know, I never wake-up emotionally scathed that I am not a Legal Interpreter. It's Ok. Why do we feel we need to prove ourselves so much as interpreters?

Compensation is definitely a favorite coping mechanism for interpreters, and for interpreting students. People, appreciate how you are wired. Accept that you have talents, and you also have other areas which do not house your best skills. Your imperfections make you human, not a bad interpreter.

– Compartmentalization –

When parts of one's values and self-awareness are compartmentalized.

We see this in the media a great deal. For example, a person in Hollywood might publicly be very critical of people who are not supportive and tolerant of all political perspectives, yet that same individual turns around and attacks someone for his/her political perspectives. They claim to believe something in one situation, then in an alternative situation they do the very thing they spoke against. They see no connection and no conflict between two completely contradicting responses. It's a classic case of compartmentalization, and sadly it's very common in America.

How does this play out in the interpreting world? For example, an interpreter might claim she feels strongly that interpreters should not chat with consumers while interpreting, however, when a Deaf consumer asks her a question when interpreting, a discussion ensues. It's an obvious contradiction and many would call it hypocrisy, but technically it's called compartmentalization. I am sure if you think hard, you can see how numerous interpreters compartmentalize their choices to justify them. Other examples of compartmentalization: Interpreters who veraciously state it is important to show up on time for a job, but when their favorite team interpreter gets reprimanded for tardiness, they make an excuse for it. Interpreters may state that teams should be supportive of one another, then miss the direct conflict with their own condemnation of interpreters. The list can go on.

We all have personal and professional rules which get stretched or broken from time to time. An interpreter who has definitively taken a stand against tardiness, then overslept one time after a particularly rough evening, has merely made a mistake. It's not good, but it happens. The compartmentalization occurs when a contradiction is blatantly ignored and/or justified with an onslaught of useless excuses. Compartmentalization negatively affects interpreting environments and deleteriously affects our relationships with both our teams and our consumers. Admit to your faults, pay attention to the soap boxes, and be sure you are not consistently ignoring your own personal and professional mandates; everyone will be much the happier.

– Projection –
The misattribution of thoughts, feelings,
or emotions onto another person

I saw an incredible example of projection with an interpreter in time gone by. She had interpreted for a complicated assignment and for a not so accurate consumer on camera. She worried that she did not accomplish the level of quality expected from her. There was no doubt that any errors which transpired were not as tragic as she had grown to believe. Everyone loved and cherished that interpreter and had confidence in her skills. Her success or failure was never given a second thought by anyone who knew of the interview. Although her agency let the impact of any error go, she could not detach from her own fears of failure. She was so frustrated with herself that she texted the boss and glibly said, "Fire me now." Of course, the boss considered the text overdramatized and sloughed off the message without a thought. Later that week, she was introduced to some people and the boss jokingly made reference to her text message, assuming the text to be null. She suddenly made a vast array of bad career choices all based on the fact that she believed people thought negatively of her. She then followed her initial bad choices with more bad choices. In the end, she nearly ended her career and severed a relationship with people who loved her because she was projecting her insecurities and her perspectives of failure on others. It was so sad. Everyone believed in her, supported her, and endorsed her, yet projection won over the open arms of those around her. It caused heartbreak, it affected the company's reputation, it affected the company's finances, it obviously affected her career, and it was all founded in a coping mechanism. Her error is not uncommon, not by a long shot. How many interpreters have made assumptions and projected their negative emotions about themselves onto others, then rode the emotional rollercoaster produced by such craziness?

Projection is not limited to personal degradation. Some interpreters will project the desire not to work; they convince their consumers that they, the consumers themselves, don't want to use an interpreter that day. In fact, the interpreters are projecting their feelings. Some interpreters think they are experienced, nearing experts in the field. They believe their methodology is the favorite of consumers. Consumer feedback can contradict, teachings can contradict, yet their perspectives of their status remain unchanged. They are projecting.

Whew! Do I see this one a lot! Yep, my performance workshops are a home to many of these projectors. I see Performance Interpreters who have been in the field for years and are faithfully loyal to the performance model advocating subtle movement and minimal expression in interpretations. I have seen Deaf people look them in the face and refute their belief system saying, "We want you to move *MORE* and have *MORE* facial expression." After these kinds of constructive suggestions from their own consumers, these loyalists will look me dead in the face and say, "The Deaf really don't want us to move." Huh? That folks is projection at its finest.

Projection has its dangers and it definitely has instigated a little havoc in the field. Whether it's projecting fears or successes, plans or emotions, it all can be quite damaging. I encourage interpreters who might fall accidentally into "projecting," to stop and find the truth. It requires trust, trust that you previously might have been unwilling to give, it requires openness you may have previously not had, but walking away from projecting only opens the door for great things in your life and your career. You might just create a happier, safer, and more effective environment for everyone.

– Displacement –

When thoughts or feelings about one person are taken out on another person.

Displacement is rampant as well in the interpreting world. For example, maybe you are mad at your husband, but you get snippy with your team interpreter. Maybe you are mad at your boss, so you act impatient with your consumer. It's a simple, yet common coping mechanism that can do a great deal of damage, and definitely not help the overall interpreting environment.

– Acting Out –

The presentation of extreme behaviors in order to compensate for alternative feelings the individual does not feel safe to express.

Interpreters who act out often opt for unhealthy behaviors like possibly yelling at their team interpreter when they are frustrated inside. The act of yelling lets them vent their emotions, and momentarily gives them emotional relief. Sometimes you see interpreters act out by falling into addictive behaviors like drinking, drugs, pornography, etc. Since they are frustrated with or emotionally battling one area of their life, they choose alternative actions to express those emotions. How does that affect the job? Well, it's not fun working with a person who has a hangover, a person who is bitter and yelling, a person who is stoned, and yes, these things do happen. Acting out does, in fact, impact the effectiveness of the interpreting environment and it clearly can affect relationships with your team, your boss, and your consumer.

Is this a comprehensive list of coping mechanisms? No. It's not intended to be. This is just a list of mechanisms I personally have seen cause damage in the field. Please understand, we all need to cope with issues in our lives. We all have problems, and yet we all have to go to work. Sometimes we choose to use healthy and positive coping skills, and other times not so much. Sometimes we have a brief relationship with these negative coping mechanisms, and sometimes our coping turns into a vicious cycle. We are human. The goal here is to acknowledge some of these coping mechanisms, understand their effect on our job, and allow us to hopefully choose better coping skills in the future.

– Healthy Emotional Management –

It's easy just to focus on the negative, but let's end on the positive. What are some positive ways to manage our emotions, and create a positive spin on our interpreting environments along with our own personal lives?

Forgiveness

I know I mentioned it before, but it's important enough to address it again here. If we let go of anger, offense, frustrations etc., whether it's with our teams, our consumers, our bosses, our friends, our spouses (well, your spouses, I am not married), our students, our animals, or even the idiotic drivers in Tennessee (ahem... just sayin'), we need to first forgive all bothersome intentional or unintentional actions on their part. In our field specifically, it makes our work environment so much more positive! When you forgive, your stress level decreases and those pesky unhealthy coping mechanisms are avoided.

Forgiveness should not just be directed towards others, we even need to forgive ourselves. I am infamous for not forgiving myself. I can list mistakes I made on the job twenty years ago. "Sam, *LET THEM GO!* The consumer doesn't even remember you were at that job most likely, much less remember the mistake you made." What if he/she does remember? Beating yourself up for years doesn't compensate for a mistake, does it? Forgiveness of others and for oneself is the first step to personal improvement.

Love

Show love and support to individuals around you. A smile, a statement of understanding, a kind word can go a long way to making an impact on your life as well as theirs. Every job is better when the interpreters show love. Don't get creepy on me now; I am not thinking anything kinky, but if a consumer is a jerk, smile. If your team is pill, offer a word of concern. If the administrator over your job is facing a bout of menopause mixed with unhealthy amounts of megalomania, run for your life, but do it with love.

Confession

Admit when you make mistakes. You are human. The stress of always defending a mistake is too great. "Yes, I interpreted that wrong." "Yes, I was late." "Yes, I didn't body shift properly." "Yes, I was in a complaining mood and let that get the best of me." Confession is powerful stuff. This entire book is full of Sam confessions. Hopefully, individuals reading it have the maturity to say, "I am not perfect either." We learn and grow predominately via our mistakes not our successes. *Mistakes are the stones upon which the paths of our lives are created.* (I just came up with that one, but I believe it's true). Accept them, admit to them, and let the stress of your failures dissipate.

Change Your Words

Be positive! I went over examples earlier so check those out once again. A little review has merit.

Joy

Your negative coping mechanisms cannot survive when there is true joy in your heart. When you have joy, true joy, it overwhelms you and you will find yourself full of life. Good things will dispel the bad, and the negative coping mechanisms find their way straight out of your mindset.

Have you ever heard that fresh and salt water cannot mix? I actually saw a real life version of this on a visit to Canada. There is a specific place where the fresh water from the land pushes into a bay with salt water. The physical conflict of the 2 types of water created a barrier. It also created a current which churned violently. People and varied forms of water craft could get caught up in the place of that conflict and face serious danger as both the fresh and the salt water fought for control over the bay. That's just like our own lives. When we find ourselves battling between the positive and the negative, the clash which ensues can cause a volatile conflict in our own minds hearts and souls. It's a sad and ineffective combination. We have to choose sides. Will we proclaim the positive or focus on the negative? Our field provides us with a vast array of opportunities to focus on the bad and avoid digging for the good. I want to challenge you to do the opposite. Proclaim the good with boldness, have joy and release your hold on the negative. In the end, you will change your work environment, yourself and maybe even a few lives.

Patience

Don't be so demanding of yourself, of your team interpreters, of your consumers, of your agencies. Have some patience. Let people walk out their own journeys to success. Give them the grace you want to be given. It makes a radical difference, and it empowers your peace!

Kindness

If your Team wants to leave 10 minutes early one day because she needs to go to the doctor, wave goodbye and wish her good health. Don't get wenchy and demand she stays the entire time. If you know it is your team's birthday, bring her a card. If you know your agency manager has been under a great deal of stress, send her flowers. Yes, it might cost you a few bucks, but isn't a person worth it? Send an anonymous e-card to someone in the field who has been hurting. When you help others, you take the focus off of yourself and *you* end up feeling better. You won't need unhealthy coping mechanisms if you can let go of you.

Self-Control

For example, maybe you don't want to do a particular job, but you committed. Do it anyway and do it with a smile. Control yourself whether it is in the area of general responsibility, attitude, or actions. Want to quit? Don't do it. Don't give yourself excuses to be mean, to complain, to be angry, or to point fingers. Not in a good mood? Listen to music that will put you in one. Don't want to smile? Smile twice as much. Want to ditch class for 30 minutes when someone says "hi" in a hall? Head straight on back. Want to cop an attitude about a request made of you which shouldn't have been made? Don't. If you have never watched Bob Newhart's version of "Stop It," jump on to YouTube and watch it today! It's hilarious and has a great point. We all need to use self-control on and off the job, and stop the bad choices which have hurt ourselves and others.

These little ideas make an amazing difference. I have used them in my life and it has radically shaped what I do and how I do it. Give it a shot! What will it hurt? You can only walk away happier.

TERZIS' TIPS!

RIIIPP!!

FEND OFF TRAGEDY!

A lot of interpreters don't realize the power of an Emergency Kit. A little preparation can fend off tragic circumstances. What is an emergency kit? Well, doctors have their doctor bags, interpreters can carry an "Interpreter Bag". An emergency kit can be the size of a backpack, or it can be much smaller, but in a perfect world it would house a wide variety of important things an interpreter might need when on the job. Suggested items to include:

- Small First-Aid Kit
- Black/White Safety Pins
- Water
- Snacks (which won't melt or perish rapidly)
- Cash
- Flashlight
- Hair Ties & Holders

- Hand Sanitizer
- Wet Wipes
- Stain Remover
- Deodorant
- Extra Make-up
- Hydrocortisone Cream
- Umbrella
- Pain Reliever
- Pocket De-Icer in Winter (in needed locales)
- Small Travel Size Body Spray
- Mouthwash Pocket Packs
- Feminine Products
- Reading Material
- Ear Buds
- Ear Plugs
- An Extra Set of Clothing
- An Extra Set of Shoes
- Etc.

These little things can really save the day! Most of these I have personally needed while on assignment at one time or another, and when I didn't have an emergency kit, I was stuck. Bra strap breaks? No problem, you have a safety pin in the Emergency Kit. Your stomach is growling and people are staring? No problem. Grab that snack. No one told you that the only parking lot available is a paid lot and accepts cash only? No problem! You have cash. Arrive at a college and you find out that the class you are interpreting is not a class on architecture but rather a class on construction where students will be constructing? No problem. Grab those ear plugs and get to it. The weather report said no rain and you are now in the middle of a downpour? OH! You must be in Nashville! (Word to the wise, *never* believe a Nashville weather report.) No problem! Umbrella is right there in hand. Get to the car and the unexpected ice storm has frozen your door shut? No biggie. Grab that pocket de-icer and you will bust into your car in no time. All of these things happen to interpreters, and a little prep can fend off tragedy.

IMPERFECT DEAF PEOPLE

Somewhere along the line we started to believe that Deaf people were perfect, that what they say "goes". At some point, interpreters started proclaiming that the Deaf were always right. When did that happen? Last time I checked, no one was perfect. It might be politically incorrect to say that Deaf individuals have faults, but guess what? They do.

– Experts on Language –
Using English

The Deaf have a tremendous challenge. English is a Level IV language, one of the toughest languages in the world to learn, and learning it isn't easy unless you hear and use it from birth. Even then, it is difficult to use correctly. There are those who beat the odds, though. I knew of one Deaf girl, in Jr. High at the time, whose reading level was unable to be charted. The school district she attended tested her English reading level with the most advanced English tests available (including PhD level English and vocabulary tests). Her skills surpassed them all. (God bless the interpreter who had to voice for her fingerspelling.) She clearly is not the norm (but if any of you know her, please have her email me. I want to meet that girl one day). Most Deaf individuals struggle a bit with English. They are not the only ones either. Many Hearing Americans struggle with English. Am I wrong, or are there millions of Americans born and raised speaking English who have horrendous English speaking skills? It's easy to find them. Just watch **Swamp People**. (Their English skills may not be noteworthy, but they have some serious *cojones* and they make a lot more money than I do!)

There are extreme situations where almost any Deaf individual will struggle with the English language. One day, I was interpreting for a college tutoring assignment. The consumer fingerspelled a word which was like 276 letters long. Ok – it wasn't that big. I am exaggerating, but it was seriously like 26 letters. I didn't interpret for that student's regular class. I didn't even speak the twisted and complicated lingo used in that particular field, and that word, I could not voice to save my life. I couldn't voice it for two reasons. The first challenge was that the student decided its enormous length was not long enough. He apparently wanted to add more letters. The already atrocious word was now dramatically increased in size (no need to emphasize the letter additions were neither needed nor wanted), and I was fresh out of psychic abilities, which would have been the only hope for me understanding what the student was saying (or trying to say). The next clearly defined bump in the road came after his third time spelling the word. I was still happily sinking into a cesspool of confusion (please note each time the student spelled it, it was a different size and configuration), and so for a final "Hail Mary," I opted to spell it out for the tutor. She said, "OH!" around letter eight and wrote it on the board. I read it, and *still* couldn't pronounce it. Yep, that's a bit of a problem now isn't it?

The concern in this scenario wasn't just the fact that the subject was unfamiliar to me (that would have helped, and so would have 30 IQ points), but an equal point of contention was the student didn't have the needed knowledge of the subject, nor the English skills to produce the word for me properly. That student wasn't perfect. His English skills were not up to the task, and clearly neither were mine. Face political incorrectness and speak the truth in love. Deaf people aren't perfect. Say it with me. It will be therapeutic for you. "Deaf people aren't perfect." Did you say it? Stop wimping out! Here's your chance. Trust me it feels good to let this bulge of contention rise to the surface and meet the fresh air. Ready? One last time. "Deaf people aren't perfect." Ah. See how refreshing that was?

So we know now that we can speak those words and no lightning bolt comes down from the sky and zaps us. Sometimes English is easy for the Deaf, sometimes it's hard. Sometimes they write like skilled

English speakers, sometimes their grammar is incomprehensible. That's just reality, and it's ok to admit. Sometimes a consumer's struggle with English makes our job hard. Sometimes we enjoy the challenge. Many of us have seen things like "E_ _ _ _ _ _ _ smart" and wisely voiced "Einstein," in the end, leaving us with an "I can conquer anything" feeling inside. Ah, yes, those are the days!

We just need to admit that some Deaf people have an expertise in English and some do not. Sometimes it's a challenge for us, and sometimes it is not. It's the reality we face as interpreters, and that reality can be one we face with a beaming smile, and with personal motivation to manage the skills and/or struggles of every consumer. We want to make the experience of using an interpreter as positive as it can be, but accepting and keeping in mind, sometimes, we just can't read minds.

Using ASL

Disclaimer: Please note, I DO believe linguistic examples of accurate ASL usage originate from the core, ASL based, non-verbal, Deaf Community.

In addition to high language and low language English speakers, there are high language and low language ASL users. To assume that Deaf individuals have a strong grasp of any signed language or system, solely because they sign is a mistake. To assume what knowledge they have of gestural communication makes them an expert in a language or system is preposterous. I love when interpreters, in an effort to be culturally supportive, say, "Well, it's their language." Whose language? You have one non-verbal Deaf Community member over here using the letter "I" when signing "I" and another using the sign for "ME". Which one is correct? Both were raised in schools for the Deaf. They both claim they are using ASL. Moment of honesty though, one is in fact using SEE.

I am not the ASL police. I will leave that to PhD linguistic professors at Gallaudet. However, I have seen signed sentences that are jumbled, awkward, and broken be touted as "hard core ASL". I have seen interpreters look at those individuals and explain the awkwardness by stating, "She is just very ASL." No, she is making no sense in all manual forms of communication. *No logical structure does not equal ASL.* It equals *bad ASL.* Americans don't get to define the correctness of English by their effort at writing English (Wow, if they did though, editing this darn book would be a much faster process!) I can use write and rong English (smile), and the Deaf can use ASL correctly or incorrectly as well.

From these examples we can see proclaiming, "The Deaf are always right" is a misnomer. Everyone can't always be right. How does that tie into our career? Sometimes your consumers are going to sign things wrong, and you are not going to understand them. Does that make you a bad interpreter? Nope! It makes you a bad psychic. True, there are many days we can take the jumbled mess handed to us and make a clearly voiced statement out of a consumer's intentions (although there is some room for argument about whether that is truly an equivalent interpretation), but if a mess comes at you, it's still a mess. The fault for the struggle in comprehension does not lie with the interpreter, it sits on the shoulders of the individual doing the signing. My audience is not responsible for my under-caffeinated communication faux pas when I teach workshops. Should I blame the attendees for not understanding a verbal blunder? No. The fault is all mine! Signing blunders have to be owned by the signer as well. Ah, isn't that nice to finally say?

Let's keep delving further into this subject. A person's language skills are not based on their nationality, or in this case, their deafness. I see ITP programs hire Deaf individuals to teach ASL classes. The problem in many cases is that they hire people who have no teaching skills, and/or have no ASL proficiency. The fallacy many ITPs capitulate to is that deafness equals knowledge and skill. It doesn't. I have seen ITPs hire ASL instructors who were SEE Signers. Really? The viewpoint? "Well, he is Deaf." And now your students are completely confused. Good decision. I love when I hear, "At least they are getting exposure to the language." Uh, people, if I want to get exposed to proper English, I wouldn't join a class taught by the guys on *Swamp People*. They might be Americans, rich Americans, gutsy Americans, even highly skilled

Americans, but their English has some room for improvement. Exposure to the language implies the person doing the exposing has a *pure and founded knowledge of...* THE LANGUAGE! That's where a lot of ITPs get lost.

What if he/she, our honorary "Deaf Joe Shmoe", has an incredible grasp of ASL? He is a great guide for the students, correct? We have a beautiful ASL Signer in our office. He is from NorCal. He went to Fremont (CSDF). He went to Ohlone College. He went to Gally. Good language influences all. He has a wonderful skill set. Everything he signs is so clear! As a language example he is *AMAZING!* As a teacher, he needs training. Why? His background in ASL doesn't make him an excellent ASL instructor. That requires training. I can't teach English. I can speak it, but I can't teach it. I don't have the training. (Let me just state I really don't want the training either.) Our resident ASL maniac may not have ended up birthed out of the head of Zeus with perfect teaching skills, but what his awesome ASL production skills did give him was a wonderful foundation on which to build. However, when he has to define what a topic marker is, or which words are modals, or how often someone should use a rhetorical question, he is lost. He knows the language, but cannot *teach* the language without direction.

I have several friends who are fluent in German. They are fluent because their families are from Germany or Austria and they have been raised speaking

German. They didn't have a profound ability to write the German language. They didn't even know how or why they would say what they said. All of them have now studied German in college. All of them have come back to me and said, "I finally *know* the language." Were they fluent before the class? Yes. Were they able to teach the class because of that fluency? NO! They would have been the first to admit it. If we admit that for foreign languages, what's the harm in admitting that when discussing ASL?

It's disappointing when standards readily understood in the Hearing world are so quickly and easily overlooked in the Deaf world. Sometimes our clients are the problem, not us. Sometimes *they* don't sign clearly. *AHH!* (Don't hit me now.) Sometimes *they* spell words wrong. *EEK!* Sometimes *they* don't use complete ASL sentences. *NO!* Sometimes *they* have so little language their ASL is incredibly choppy. *PLEASE NO MORE!* Sometimes *they* even use the wrong sign. *TOO MUCH!* Deaf people are not perfect. They are just people. So clearly, sometimes ITPs need to change their philosophies regarding instructor choices, and dare I say, we in the field need to get honest about the language capabilities of our friends, clients, and co-workers. Let's show respect to ASL's greatest living language examples, but let's be forthright and admit that some Deaf individuals just use bad ASL. Let's avoid jumping on the political band wagon claiming they are using "true ASL". Honesty is always empowering.

– Experts on the Culture –

I was raised with two family cultures, Greek and Southern. That doesn't make me an expert on being Greek or being Southern. I was raised in Southern California. I definitely get beach bound Southern Californians, but they make the most sense to me because I have spent my life immersed in long haired, scruffy, sand infused, s'more laced, surf culture. (I needed an excuse to include s'mores in my book. Found one.)

My mom was from Arkansas. She had an accent. She knew how to cook fried food. Her family all wore plaid, lived on the same street, and were very *VERY* involved in each other's lives. My cousins were even married... to each other. Mom's high school was the second Southern school in the U.S. to be integrated which means mom's senior year went down in infamy landing her school in national news, in a starring role as the topic of a made-for-TV movie, and most importantly, noted in the Billy Joel song "We Didn't Start the Fire". For better or for worse from family to history, mom was a Southerner, in all senses of the word. However, I didn't see it. I never noticed any accent. We ate more California style foods than we ever did biscuits and gravy, and outside of the 70's I never donned plaid. Mom had acclimated to the South... SoCal that is. We lived our lives with no distinction from any other San Diegans. The fact is, I might be Southern (by adoption) but I am no expert on the South. I moved to Nashville and couldn't figure out what the heck a "buggie" was, what on earth "washing powder" was used for, why every traffic light at any stage of traffic control was considered a "red light;" I am just not an expert. To say I am because my family is from the South, and I now live in the South is outlandish. I was exposed to it, but I will never claim to be the voice of Southerners.

So what is the implication here? A person's deafness does not establish him/her as an expert on Deafness any more than my Southern roots and exposure to the South makes me an expert on the culture here. The Deaf can speak to their own experiences. If someone was raised Oral, I doubt his/her understanding of non-verbal Deaf Culture is as proficient as some may claim, not without training in that area. If someone was raised fully immersed in Deaf Culture, he/she can't speak to all types of deaf experiences as there are so many aids and communication styles to go along with deafness these days, and each combination modifies the experience. Can they speak to it some, YES! I can speak to the culture of the South and the Greeks *some*. Are they experts? Maybe they are, or maybe not. It depends on the person, his/her background, and the training of the individual.

The moral of this story is that before you endorse the expertise of any individual, evaluate his/her skills, background, experiences, and training. When you do find one, it's a wonderful thing.

– Admit Their Issues –

The mentality that, "Deaf people are always right" has been pervasive and has leaked into other aspects of Interpreter/Deaf interaction. Some individuals claim to be Deaf when they are not. I have friends and professors who have fallen into that category. Some Deaf individuals are law breakers, or just jerks. Although when we are on the job, we are just there to do a job, and consumer analysis has to be limited to job related issues such as practical and linguistic accessibility. Off the job though, I see interpreters take that same pedestal of perfection and place it under the consumers with whom they interact in public. Let's stop and note, Deaf people (or ones claiming to be Deaf) come in all shapes and sizes, and their imperfections do not need to be so rigorously ignored or protected.

There are lots of reasons issues are not acknowledged or confronted. Many times our lack of directness with these individuals comes down to the fact that it is politically incorrect to concede to the gaffes of Deaf individuals, even in a friendship. I can't say I agree, although I too find myself playing into the game of political correctness. I think it's better to acknowledge truth, call a spade a spade, and admit to the humanity of our Deaf friends as well as ourselves. You see, people, all people, have issues. People are people! I believe treating people with honesty is a sign of respect. Sometimes the most respectful thing you can do in your private time with friends, mentors, etc., is let them be people, human, error filled, and not put them on the pedestal of faultlessness.

I have a dear friend who, for years, signed AGO like ONE-YEAR-AGO. She would sign "I met him a week ago" like "I met him for one week a year ago." Finally, after years of watching this, I intervened. Why did I wait years? It's politically incorrect to correct the Deaf, even friends. I decided to wave goodbye to politics and just be a friend. She actually was a bit embarrassed that no one had ever corrected her. It was a lot like walking out of a bathroom with a piece of toilet paper stuck to our shoe. It's better to have someone mention it and get it off our foot immediately, than cruise through a restaurant and out the door with the TP still fully intact. That's what she felt like. It would have been better if one of her friends or interpreters had mentioned something years before. Instead everyone honored the holy unwritten code. Never correct the Deaf.

"It's not our place." "It's their language." "We have no right." I have heard it all, and thought it all. I would never correct a *consumer* unless I had a very comfortable and longstanding relationship with him/her. Hear me when I say, I am **NOT** advocating for correction of your consumers. However, I think it's important to acknowledge that Deaf people are PEOPLE, fallible people. They might have personal issues, they might have language issues, but there is no person in America who doesn't have issues.

– A Little Known Secret That Blessed Me –

I was chatting with a Deaf person one day, and he told me something that was life changing. He said, "Oh, Deaf people don't understand a ton of fingerspelled words. We just fake it." Huh? He said, "Yeah, we just don't want to ask for things to be repeated so we act like we understand and ignore it." I couldn't believe it. I started asking other Deaf friends and consumers in all kinds of locations across America and they all said the same thing! It was awesome! I finally didn't feel like I had to beat myself up if I missed a single fingerspelled word. Honestly, I am human. Sometimes I can't remember the English word for "mailbox" or "cabinet" or even "door" (I need more sleep) so understanding a second language on a day filled with brain flatulence can be comical. When I found out that even Deaf people had moments like that, I felt so empowered. Deaf people are human too!

– How It Changed Me –

When I eventually brought all these truths together it changed me. I realized that Deaf people weren't always infallible. When they ask for something like ASL and they clearly communicate in and prefer PSE, give them what they need and prefer rather than merely administering what they ask for. In the end, they always leave thanking me. When I realized they weren't faultless and often made lexical or syntactical errors, I started watching for their meaning and voiced what I knew they meant instead of what they said. The response from all consumers has been amazing. When I realized that they didn't understand every fingerspelled word, I started making sure my fingerspelling was sometimes slightly slower and even clearer, and they thanked me for it. When I could tell the consumers struggled to understand the material, I began to expound more, and the feedback was inspiring. Learning that Deaf people are just *people* was a radical shift in my thinking, and it has positively impacted my career and the education my interpreting students receive. For many of you, this concept is not new, and many or all of these concepts might be ones you have long since adopted, yet for the vast majority of interpreters with whom I interact, this will be a new bright light in a mentally gray world.

TERZIS' TIPS!

PLAN FOR THE "UNPLANABLE"

DISCLAIMER:

This TERZIS TIP needs backstory to validate the lessons I learned, lessons which I now feel the need to pass on to you. So settle in for one heck of a story about a day I will never ever forget... and tips I hope will impact your life (or at least make you laugh).

I am **NOT** a test taker. I am a paranoid mess when it comes to taking tests, so taking the RID was something I fully planned to put off as long as possible. I came from a generation of interpreters who would not even consider taking the RID until they had been in the field for five years. That was fine with me! After many more than five years I decided I needed to "put my big girl pants on", hunker down, and take the exam. Eww.

I took the written test far away from my home, in the land of ice skating, great cheese, and Kopp's Frozen Custard (some of you just drooled), the frigid northern city of Milwaukee. I have no idea why. I think I had a friend in the area and thought it would be an excuse to see the town and treat myself to a little fun once the test had ended. It went ok. I passed, and I vaguely remember getting to see the town. All seemed well. This gave me false hope that tests taken under this system would always pan out well. After I put off the performance test for many more years (don't judge me!), I finally decided it was time to face the music and take the next exam.

I had it all planned out; I would make a fun weekend of it. It worked the first time. I would leave my house early in the morning, schedule the test for late afternoon, drive from Nashville to Little Rock, Arkansas (six and a half hours), take the test, see some family, and then drive home. Sounds good doesn't it? Ah, yes. So good.

Let's rethink this with a little more logic. I am not a test taker. I planned to drive a significantly long distance and take an exceptionally demanding assessment. At the time, the passing rate for the CT was 42%. Incredible Stress = STRIKE 1. I am not a morning person yet somehow it seemed logical to decide to get up really early in order to drive to the exam. Functional Blow = STRIKE 2. I decided to take the exam at a long distance location, the drive being over six hours. Did I plan to arrive the day before? Nope. Exhausted = STRIKE 3. I planned to see my Arkansas family who I have not seen in 10 + years. I was really nervous as many members of my family were anti-Californian. I found out one of the more daunting members of my family would be stopping by (probably to check out the Californian). Fear and Intimidation = STRIKE 4. This is going well. That was the good part. This is where my dramatic tale takes a significant turn for the worse.

::: Dramatic music please! :::

I got up early that morning, panicked of course, and left for the exam. I thought I was so careful. I left a 90 minute window for traffic issues or unexpected wrong turns. Surely, I would not need any more time than that! Sounds so wise doesn't it? It did to me. Back then we took two exams, the CI and the CT. I decided to take the CT first. I took the exam back during the Clinton administration. That didn't work well for me.

I got in the car to start my trek to Arkansas. I was nervous and stressed, but I did everything I could to make the experience as positive as it could be. First, my radio was broken, so I brought a boom box. I had bought new batteries from a dollar store so I would have music all the way to Little Rock. (A+ for preparation, right?) Then, I made my plans with my family, so in theory I would have something to anticipate. (More prep, it's going well. Yea for Sam!) I wore my ideal interpreter attire. (Check. I was set! Such a happy fantasy.)

Remember my remark about Clinton? Well, I arrived in Memphis, TN and the freeway was shut down. Why, do you say? Clinton. Any ounce of love I had for that man ended that day. Clinton was on his way to Arkansas to bury a Senator. Fabulous. I appreciate the political support he showed his governmental representatives, but did it have to be on the exact day and time I needed access to the same freeway? His 35+ car motorcade (just a guess) needed complete and safe access to the freeway, so the entire freeway closed as he and his deceased Senator cruised on by. I prepped for a lot, but not a Presidential motorcade. Well, I was fine. I had an hour and a half built into my schedule, remember?

Once the freeway had been shut down for 45 minutes, I started to stress. We kept waiting. Eventually, I heard spewing coming from the front seat. "What the heck was that?" I turned and looked at my radio and battery acid from my new dollar store batteries was spurting out the back, onto the seat. "WHAT? OMG!" I grabbed the radio and picked it up and acid started pouring out of my doomed box, into (you know there had to be more) the shoes I had brought to wear to the exam! Now my shoes are an acid filled death trap. OK, let's keep a positive perspective. Those shoes did in fact protect the seat... some.

I should have gotten out, walked around the car, opened the door, and pulled the radio out of the passenger seat; I mean, we weren't going anywhere. Hindsight is 20/20 they say. Instead, I picked up the radio and crossed from the passenger seat, crossed over the gear shift, and out the driver side door. One problem, I forgot to move my other hand out of the way. The radio crossed over my lap and acid poured all over my hand and arm. Yea! Acid burns! If that wasn't enough, I added to my suffering by then trying to wipe off the acid using my other hand. (I know it doesn't appear that way, but I really do have an IQ above four.) So, I was stressed, panicked, itching, burning, and apparently I had no shoes. I did, however, have damaged upholstery. This isn't going well.

I popped open the trunk and saw that I had grocery bags. I put the radio into the bags and put it in the trunk. Then I saw, *WATER!* (Ooo, that will help.) My theory: the acid was now on both of my hands and water would surely wash away the acid and reduce the pain and itching. Right then, if I had a guardian angel, he was probably screaming "Don't Do IT!!" Either that, or he was on a coffee break, downing a mocha at Starbucks.

I picked up the water and poured it on my hands and BAM! They were scalded. What before was burning and itching was now BURNING LIKE FIRE and ITCHING INCESSANTLY! I didn't know what to do. I grabbed my acid filled shoes, poured out the acid on the ground, put them in the trunk, and then tried to conjure up a solution to the imminent doom which approached.

I saw a cop in the front of the traffic. IDEA: Cops have first aid kits (and clearly I wasn't carrying an Interpreter Emergency Kit). I pulled out of the line of cars and drove to the officer, knocked on his window and asked for medical assistance. I said, "Sir, I poured acid on my hands and they are really burning. Can you help me?" He said, "No." I said, "You must have something. It's really hurting!" No joke, he held up a donut napkin and said, "I have this." (Thanks dude. Glad my tax dollars are going toward paying your well-deserved salary.) I grabbed the wannabe napkin and went back to my car. What was positive about this cop interaction was that I was then located at the front of the line of traffic. Ten minutes later, the freeway opened up and I was the first to jump on the road to Little Rock. This whole freeway incident really impeded my schedule, and looking at the time, I was already going to be late for the exam. Bye-Bye 90 minute window.

I pulled in behind Clinton and his buddies. Apparently, the target speed for this motorcade was about 45 mph. At this point, I was fit to be tied. People had pagers then, not cell phones, so there was no calling for help or to warn the LTA (Licensed Test Administrator) I was annoyed that my tax dollars were spent not only to withhold medical care for acid burns, but now apparently with the sole objective of torturing me en route to my exam. My hands were burning, my radio was out of commission, my shoes are ruined, my passenger seat was injured, and now I am driving 45 mph behind a Presidential motorcade. I could feel that I was going to take someone out. I was going to go to jail.

Right in front of me was an ambulance. I was trapped behind him for at least 45 minutes. I kept thinking, "Is it illegal to pull over the Clinton Motorcade ambulance and ask for medical assistance? That ambulance is filled with medicines which can help me." I doubt I have ever pondered anything harder, before or since. I decided jail time would make me sad, so I opted to stare longingly at the ambulance until finally the motorcade pulled off the freeway. In retrospect, I bet the Senator in question was in that ambulance. Yikes! Waving down that ambulance could have been bad. Darn motorcade.

Once the freeway was open, I pulled off at a truck stop to try and do something for my hands. In my final stroke of complete and utter genius, I washed my hands with not only water, but soap! Ouch! That didn't go well either. Nope, not at all.

I got on the road and headed as fast as I could to the university. The very kind LTA was closing up when in I walked. I told him who I was and he said, "Well, there you are. We were wondering what happened to you." I asked him, "Do you want to know what happened?" He had no chance for escape; it came bucketing out. The entire story propelled out my pie-hole like the forcibly dispelled water out of the Hoover Dam. He looked at my pitiful self and said, "I think they would understand if you asked for an excuse and took it another time." Geez, I hope so! I said, "NO! After all this, I am probably going to fail and I don't care; at least I will know what the test looks like." I took it. By the time I got to part three of the exam, all strength in me was lost. I was done. Yep! Done... D-O-N-E... DONE! But I finished the test.

What did I learn from this experience?

1. Never drive extremely far to an exam you are going to take the same day.
2. If you are going to travel to locations outside your area, make sure you arrive the day before and stay near the exam site.
3. Never plan stressful experiences around your test (e.g.: meeting intimidating family members after a decade).
4. Always bring an alternative set of clothes *and* shoes, just in case.
5. Always give yourself an enormous amount of lead time when driving significant distances.
6. Never buy cheap batteries.
7. Never use water on acid burns.
8. And never drive behind a Presidential motorcade when you are in a hurry.

So, did I pass? Not all of it, but I passed 2/3 of it; Part 3 took me down as expected. I followed these new found rules when I took the test the next time, and I did just fine. Now, to that incredibly kind LTA at the university in Arkansas, the man who graciously managed my emotional breakdown that day, thank you. Whoever you are I owe you one.

DO UNTO THE COMMUNITY

Have you ever thought about how inconvenient or even difficult it is to be Deaf? It's tough! Every week I think about little things which for me are so simple, yet for the Deaf can be so much more complicated. Have you ever dropped something and only knew it had fallen because you heard it hit the floor? Have you ever been running around on a busy rainy day and were incredibly thankful for the ability to order your Starbucks coffee via the drive-thru? Have you ever wanted to try a new church, attend a play, or go to a concert without any major planning in advance? Have you thought how nice it is to drive and listen to the radio, your iPod, an audio book, a sermon, or some self-help lecture? Isn't it nice to have a conversation in a car without having to look at the person next to you? When you have situations which require phone interaction such as re-booking a flight, or resolving an issue with your bank, isn't it lovely that you can speak directly to the operator, or agent? Isn't it nice that you can hear someone calling your name from a distance? True, there are accommodations. Times have changed. Thank God for VRS, accessibility laws, and even voice software apps which can be downloaded so ordering at a drive-thru is a greater possibility. How awesome that we have captioning, and text messaging, and alert devices. Being Deaf today in America is much *much* easier than it was 40 years ago. Our world, in many ways, has improved.

Accessibility and opportunities for the Deaf have improved, but there are still challenges. I have had friends who are frustrated because, even in the Bible Belt, they couldn't find an accessible home church. I have friends who have had some very difficult or emotional experiences with interpreters in the past, and now face chronic anxiety because of the skill or gender of past interpreters. A teenager once said to me, "I can't flirt through you." How profound! A male teen flirting through an adult woman does lose some impact. Following a movie is easier for me, following a lecture is easier for me, English is easier for me, and it's all because I can hear. I have pondered so many of the unique challenges of Deafness, and I decided to respond by attempting to make the experience of being Deaf as positive as it can be. Simple actions from an interpreter can sometimes bring results which will last a lifetime.

What are some simple steps we can take? Let's look at a few and see how we can go above and beyond our base goal of translation to make the experience of being Deaf the best it can be.

– Be Kind –

Being Deaf is hard enough. Being deaf while using an interpreter with a poopy attitude is even less enjoyable. So, be kind. Walk in and say "Hi." Avoid being rude. Smile. Keep a positive vibe while you are on the job. Avoid all the negative attributes which are often associated with Sign Language Interpreter horror stories. Make being around you a positive experience for all, especially your Deaf Consumers.

– Make a Way –

When I was an educational interpreter in my 20's I realized that Hearing students felt intimidated by interpreters and wouldn't talk to my students because they had to talk through me. I decided to see if I could open a few doors, so, I started experimenting. I set one particular class as my target. I began throwing out a few compliments to a girl as we entered the class. That simple effort opened the door for more questions. The teen started asking me about sign language and Deaf people. I was able to use that as a springboard to explain what she needed to know in order to interact with my student. Almost immediately she engaged my student directly, and they had an incredible semester of interaction. This successful experiment started by breaking down the intimidation barrier known as, "The ominous interpreter in the classroom". What I found is if I make myself accessible to the Hearing, they are far less likely to avoid the Deaf. It doesn't require a lot of time or a lot of effort, but it works like a charm. I have seen these tiny attempts at dissolving fears change the lives of our consumers time and time again.

– Empower Knowledge –

A lot of interpreters interpret info, but make the experience of following a lecture or a class difficult. For example, a lot of interpreters point at who is talking, then sign what is said. Yeah... let's think about this. If you are in a room with 30 hearing people and you point into a crowd, unless the Deaf person has super human powers, how is he/she going to know who is talking? If name signs are not known, try adding, "Blue shirt," "Long hair," "NY hat," etc., then pointing. I have found when I do this Deaf people are far more likely to follow what is being said and by whom.

Empowering knowledge can come in the form of clarifications about sounds, emotions, or vocal patterns. Avoid leaving out easily recognizable information such as rain, cracking of the voice, or a stutter. For example, an interpreter can body shift and state, "GERMAN ACCENT". I can't tell you the number of times I have done that and the consumer has looked at me and said, "No one has ever told me he was German before!" Then I see the consumers eagerly discuss their new found piece of knowledge. Sometimes these additional tidbits are life-savers in an interpretation. The consumers suddenly realize why interpreters have been unable to understand the speaker, why certain unique phrases are used, why the speaker makes certain references, or even why responses from the crowd are formed.

Deaf consumers often feel empowered when the speaker refers back to the auxiliary sound information, and because the interpreter dove in for an explanation early on, they are already aware of the speaker's cold, the trouble he was having with the microphone, the baby that won't stop crying, or the horrendous sound the A/C makes. Interpreters often believe that the Deaf only want the base info, and sometimes that is true. I have had one consumer who prefers no superfluous information. She is low language and prefers to process as little as possible. For her, baseline information is ideal. I have discovered, though, that she is not my most common consumer. The Deaf often want to know and understand everything Hearing people do. So unless you run across that rare case of someone who only wants the fundamentals, take the time and tell them someone has an accent, if someone's voice indicates he/she is nervous, or perhaps if a speaker's hand keeps playing with the keys in his pocket. Let them know if a speaker's voice is distinct, such as incredibly low or incredibly high. Leave no auditory stone unturned. I have made this a feature of my interpreting for years, and I have been thanked more than you can imagine.

Are there times when it is far better to avoid explanations of personal or environmental sounds? Yes, of course. Use your judgment. You have to evaluate your consumers and the particular situation in which you offer your services. If the verbalized material is moving along too fast, if the Deaf consumer is clearly one who won't understand, if sound description becomes distracting or offensive, drop it. You have to feel out those moments, and even blatantly ask for preferences. Make sure everyone gets served to the best of your ability and all will be well.

Expansion also helps empower knowledge. For example, if a person quotes something you know is taken from a Billy Joel song, body shift and express that information. If you are interpreting and a comment is made about moonwalking, use your classifiers to show how moonwalking appears rather than just referencing the name. If someone pipes up with "Live long and prosper" in a college lecture and you are enlightened enough to know that the quote is taken from Star Trek (which is of course undeniably the greatest television series of all time) you can expand by using one hand to express the famous Vulcan gesture, and the other to interpret the phrase. Most Deaf individuals may not recognize the wording but almost all of them will recognize the hand-shape. Expansion empowers knowledge and comprehension, and when I have used it, I have never seen a negative response.

– Advocate... With a Smile –

Advocating for your consumers is critical. We need to make sure there is a good line-of-sight, that the interpreter can be seen, that the Deaf have note-takers, and accessibility is available as needed to understand what is being interpreted. Interpreters often make these requests with an attitude. This negativity not only reflects badly on the consumer, but on future interpreters for that assignment. Please don't be fussy with the people of whom you are making requests.

Advocating with a smile also means avoiding spouting the ADA (Americans with Disabilities Act) at every turn. Quoting the law causes offenses to be built up and Hearing people don't like being threatened. The ADA, IDEA (Individuals with Disabilities Education Act), and PL 94-142 are your last stops on the road to advocacy, not your first. The minute you whip those out, people get mad, so leave them in your back pocket until absolutely necessary. It keeps your Hearing consumers and your Deaf consumers interacting in a positive manner as long as possible.

On that same smiley road to advocacy I must mention that the CPC doesn't come with a tenet insisting on rudeness. I might have missed a recent update, so I guess there is a chance I am wrong here, but last time I checked I found no requirement to act "wenchy". One of the worst episodes relayed to me is one I mention in my performance workshops. An interpreter on stage was approached by an artist who obviously intended to interact with her on some level. Because she viewed the CPC (or at that time the "Code of Ethics") as requiring complete anonymity, she felt the proper course of action was to stop the artist. When he approached her, she then turned her back on him. Wasn't she advocating for the interpreter's anonymity and Deaf audience member's equality? Of course not! The thousands of people in the audience that night were unaware of the goals of our Code. They didn't see that action and suddenly stop and think, "I bet she was wanting to remain anonymous on stage so that the Deaf were in no way acknowledged as being different than the Hearing audience members." Nope, I can guarantee that didn't cross their minds. I can guarantee that didn't cross the mind of the artist either. What did cross their minds is that she was being rude. I am sure the Deaf felt so fulfilled by her advocacy efforts (sarcasm). How much damage did that little foray into self-righteousness cause? First, she brought the entire energy of the concert down, and put a damper on the whole night. If that isn't enough, she embarrassed the artist and the Deaf consumers. Additionally, the consumers will likely not want another interpreter at a concert, so she has impacted their accessibility. In addition to that, the artist now wants nothing to do with interpreters or Deaf access. Great job lady. I don't know who that interpreter was, but I can see the damage she likely caused with that one action, and it makes me sad. Advocating for the CPC is an excellent endeavor. Please remember, though, to do it with a smile, at appropriate times, and without threats. In the end, *positive interaction breeds positive results* and everyone wins.

– Avoid - "It's Not My Job" –

I have heard horror stories of interpreters who love the phrase, "It's not my job." I heard about an interpreter who was sitting right next to the light switch and the instructor asked her to flip it and she said, "It's not my job" which then forced the instructor to walk across the room, lean over her, and flip the switch. Literally, she would have burned under a single calorie had she lifted her precious finger to flip the darn switch. She irritated the instructor, embarrassed the consumer, and gave interpreters a bad name all in one fell swoop. Yea. Should you run errands for your instructor? No. Refuse to touch a light switch placed only an inch from your head? Maybe that one is a tad extreme.

I know interpreters want to define their role and manage expectations, but there is no need for extreme boundaries or discourteousness. If you are going to get a Coke, and the Deaf person asks you to buy him/her one too, then hands you the money, it is not necessary to be fussy and say, "That's not my job." Some people want to call that maintaining boundaries, but I personally think it is being rude. Be kind to Deaf people, people! The loss of 10 seconds of your life to hit the button twice for a second Coke isn't going to make a radical impact on your personal boundaries or life choices. It's just a Coke. Flipping a light switch is not going to open the door for you running to Wal-Mart on break for the teacher. It's just a light switch. Kindness will go a long way towards building bridges for future accessibility and relationships.

– Make an Offer –

I know some interpreters who are so stringent about boundaries, if they walk out of an assignment and pull out a stick of gum, they won't offer one to their consumers. You don't need to offer them $100 or a ride home, but you can offer them a stick of gum. Little things like that can really put a smile on someone's face, and I think it's nice to make someone smile.

What other offers can be made? How many times have I heard this from college students? "Can you just run with me over to the __ office for a sec? I need to ask [so-and-so] a question." If you have the time, I believe it's kind to say, "Yes, I'd be happy to." Maybe you are only paid for a class, but the fact is that if you were Deaf wouldn't you want the interpreter to be willing to take 10 minutes and help you out? Now, if you are busy, have another job, etc., "I can't," seems quite appropriate. However, if you have the time, what's the harm? I always stop and think, "If the roles were reversed, what would I want from my interpreter?"

– Be Inconvenienced –

I worked with a Deaf/Blind guy once who used a disabled ride service. Being Deaf has its challenges, being Deaf *and* blind is really tough. When we walked out of an appointment, the ride service had not arrived for his pick-up. I could have left him there. Technically, my job was over, but I knew he rarely had someone to chat with, so I opted to wait and chat a bit about superficial things until his ride made an appearance and I knew he was safely en route home. Was it inconvenient? Yes, but it blessed him, and helped him to feel comfortable in a strange environment. We didn't discuss the appointment, we didn't discuss his life problems, but that little act of service brightened his day, and I saw him safely get on his bus. I know we are all busy, and sometimes that type of inconvenience isn't possible, but when it is, give it a shot. You never know the impact it can make.

– Volunteer –

I know some interpreters who are vigilantly against volunteering to interpret. In their minds, pro-bono work is a "no-no". People, we have a skill that Deaf people need. We should get paid for our work, but sometimes the Deaf do things that require an interpreter yet there is no budget and no legal requirement for the provision of an interpreter. Often paying $1200 for two interpreters to show up at a free health workshop open to the public is a little out of a consumer's financial reach. Why is it that we can't allow ourselves to be inconvenienced a little?

A Deaf individual wanted to attend a private sports camp one year. The set-up of the camp was such that legally the camp was not required to provide an interpreter. The size also made it financially impossible. Yet, a Deaf person wanted to better themselves by attending the camp. When the information floated across my line of sight, I couldn't ignore the request. If I were Deaf, I would want someone to inconvenience themselves to help me. So I did. It wasn't easy. It was incredibly long, it came at an incredibly inconvenient time for me personally, but when I put myself in the shoes of that consumer, I thought about what I would have wanted. I dug up another volunteer to replace me at a certain point and the consumer was able to be served. Sure, I was justified in saying, "No." In fact, I had a great deal of rationalization which made "No" very tempting indeed. My schedule was a serious problem, the length was a definite problem, the subject matter wasn't the easiest, and it was an hour away. I went anyway. The consumer was incredibly appreciative. I knew that she would remember that sacrifice for years, and use the info she learned daily. I wasn't just impacting her life and career, I was impacting the lives of the people she would train in the future. In the grand scheme of things, isn't that sacrifice worth it? Volunteer on occasion! A small gesture of service can make an incredible difference.

I believe we can and should do more than just dispel information. A small act of kindness, a tiny gesture, a sacrifice on your part can make the experience of being Deaf a better one. It can make the experience of using an interpreter a better one. It can inspire. It can change lives. Next time you sit down on a job, consider your interaction with your consumers, the next time you consider your personal boundaries, the next time you consider your service, think about how you would like to be served if you were Deaf. "Do unto others..." You never know how much of a difference you can make.

TERZIS' TIPS!

DEVELOP A THICK SKIN

Almost no advice I could give would be more important than this: the reality is that people will complain about you. It may be that you have made a mistake, or it could be that they are whiners. You have to develop a thick skin in this field. Sometimes people will get frustrated with you because of a genuine concern. Sometimes they will get frustrated with you because the wind is blowing. Don't take people's viewpoints personally. Evaluate the complaint, see if it has any merit, bring it before a trusted mentor, make changes if necessary, and let it go.

– Thick Skin with Interpreters –

During one season of my career, I landed smack dab in the middle of political interpreting, which I hated. My consumer loved me and wanted me for every meeting. Since the need to pay the rent won over my desire to stay out of the political arena, I accepted the jobs time and time again. One day, a team was placed with me on a lengthy assignment. She was certified at a high level, so in theory she was a good interpreter. One problem... the consumer didn't like her style. During one very formal meeting, she unexpectedly stopped, looked straight at us both and said, "Get out of the chair, Sam replace her now! You interpret the rest of the day!" Wow. What am I supposed to do now? A thousand things ran through my mind. I was completely overwhelmed. Do I sit and interpret all day by myself? Do I fight for this team interpreter? Is the consumer the final say on who interprets? Do I run screaming from the room? I was in my twenties, so I was really unsure of how to handle that particular piece of drama. The meeting was important and fast paced so there was no opportunity to have a discussion about the situation, so I kept my mouth shut, I sat down, and interpreted. That interpreter never spoke to me again. My team interpreter that day apparently held quite a mighty grudge too. I heard she made publicly denigrating my name, a part time job. She had grabbed one of those unhealthy coping mechanisms and was going to town, literally. Had I taken up personal offense, it would have dug into me for years. Deep down inside she was just embarrassed; she didn't hate me. I needed a thick skin with her, realizing her verbal assaults were directed at me because of her own embarrassment and pain. She needed a thick skin with our consumer that day. Sounds like a perfect moment to tackle that subject.

– Thick Skin with the Deaf –

Sometimes the Deaf will complain about you for a wide variety of reasons. Some might be valid and you need to consider those. If a Deaf person says, "It's hard to understand your fingerspelling," don't be offended. Work on it. If a consumer says, "Can you use more ASL?" It's all good, do your best to add more. Now, if a Deaf person pipes up with a comment like, "Could you please dress more provocatively for my viewing pleasure," go ahead and get offended. I doubt that's going to happen though. The Deaf may have valid skills, habits, or tendencies they want you to change. Those suggestions could be useable and they could make you a better interpreter. If they are not, and you have just been blessed with a sourpuss for a consumer, keep on smiling and don't take any garbage to heart.

Sometimes you cannot alter yourself to meet their preferences. A deaf person may not prefer my presence on a medical job because I am not male. Why should I get angry about that? I had an oral Deaf friend mention that she prefers a different curly headed Nashville Terp over me for Oral Interpreting work. Why? That interpreter has bigger lips than those embellishing my Greek/Lebanese face. The other interpreter is far easier to lip-read. Hey, it's not my fault. Blame my birth parents. Maybe a Deaf consumer wants someone else for Celine Dion because that interpreter and Celine are both a size 0. I am not. It's all good! I might like Carrie Underwood and you like Beyonce. Does that mean Beyonce is worse than Carrie Underwood or vice versa? No! She is just different. It's all just about personal preferences.

So fellow Terps, develop a thick skin. Not everyone is going to like you. Trust me, after reading this book, I will have all kinds of people scowling when they think of me. Silly them. I am a nice person, and although this book is a bit frank, I only want our field to grow, and for all of us to be at our very best. The fact is, we have to live and work without the emotional and psychological bondage of offense. Instead we need to maintain a spirit of forgiveness and mutual support. If we do, there will be a lot less drama in the field and many more smiles. Sounds good to me!

REMEMBERING WHY WE DID THIS

Do you remember why it is you decided to get involved with the Deaf in the first place? For some of you it was based on the fact that you grew up around Deafness and needed a job. For so many of us, though, we just thought sign language was *cool*. Sometimes I think we need to stop and go back to the old days and remember what it was that drew us into this field on day one. I have been in it for 23 years now, and truthfully the wide eyed eager Sam has waned. Fellow interpreters, especially seasoned interpreters, I honestly think, we need to get back to the days when there was far less drama, and ASL was just a pretty language.

– Remembering –

I remember when I couldn't wait to get around Deaf people so I could sign. When I was just entering the big bad world of Interpreting, I attended a church with a Deaf ministry in San Diego. Everyone there used ASL, and they all signed a whole lot faster than I did. How many hours did I stare blankly at those flying hands, wondering why people were laughing? Some days I left church having only recognized a handful of sentences. I am sure the, "What the heck are you saying? Yikes! Fake it Sam, fake it!" look on my face was hard to miss. Poor little receptively disabled thing. Makes you want to hug my neck, huh? By the end of the summer, things were much better; I had made a lot of wonderful friends and I could even understand them. Years later, one of the interpreters in that church moved to Nashville and we served as team interpreters. She looked at me when we sat down on our first assignment together, a decade plus later and said, "You will always be 18 to me." I get it! Goodness, was I green back in the day? Her words made me feel 18 again mind you, and her presence freaked me out enough to make it a less than perfect semester of Sam interpreting. I do however look back and remember those old days with fondness.

I remember when a group of Deaf friends took me to a Deaf Camp in Los Angeles. I was extraordinarily terrified! There were just so many hands forming words and sentences at lightning speed. The terror went from manageable to overwhelming as soon as I arrived, so I refused to even get out of the van! They left me there. Haha! I eventually mustered up the courage to make it out the door, and it changed my life. I made lifelong friends at that camp, and I made a slew of memories which will remain close to my heart forever. That simple weekend shaped me as an interpreter and an instructor. So many thanks to those I met and interacted with up in the mountains that weekend.

I remember Ray. Oh, dear Ray. Ray used to call me through the Relay service and either torture the operators with his deviant conversations or torture me with his salacious lies. That man made me laugh... a lot. My younger days in college and in the field wouldn't have been the same without him. Wherever you are Ray, THANK YOU! Couldn't have done it without you.

I remember my second music competition. I decided to interpret the song "Hero" by Mariah Carey. It was a great song, and my additive of set pieces made it even more dramatic. The theatre was a concert hall so the floor was slick and low, and the seats raked high above the stage. I had placed a black bathroom rug on the floor to hold my computer chair in position. I began the song, sitting backwards, dramatically lifting my head for the first words of Mariah's lovely ballad. I started to sign with passion. I got up, carefully swung my leg off of the chair, walked to the side, first turning left, then turning right. I worked the song interpreting with every ounce of emotion and facial expression I could muster, then ended sitting backwards in the chair again, head bowing down slowly and arms moored around the back of the chair for my dramatic close. Doesn't it sound nice? Yeah, it was... until the music faded and disaster struck!

The lights went out, and thank God the people liked the song and clapped very loudly for an extended period of time. Why? Because I couldn't get off the chair! The computer chair's hydraulic base had popped up. My short little 5' 1" body had with it short stubby legs, and those legs were now dangling above the floor. PROBLEM! The applause continued. I leaned over and streeeeeetched my legs. Only one toe could reach the floor. It was not going well. PROBLEM! I used that toe to push, hoping to get enough leverage to dislodge me from the chair. Didn't work. PROBLEM! What I did do was accidently push myself off of the rug and launched myself across the stage, sideways! PROBLEM! The applause continued. I tried to use the other toe on the other side of my body to push off again. Across the stage I went with lighting speed. PROBLEM! The applause continued. I was thoroughly appreciative of the crowd support because I was in a BAD situation. In addition, I was completely humiliated by the fact I couldn't get off a chair! I never saw 5' 1" as a disability prior to that moment, but clearly it must have been. There was no hope. I was trapped! I did the only thing I knew to do. As the applause started to die down, and the hope of success at extricating my flaccid lower limbs from their helpless role in this scenario died with the applause, I used all the oomph I could muster, threw my body weight sideways and cast that chair to the floor. ::: SLAM! ::: Ouch. I grabbed the hydraulically deficient chair and the minimally helpful carpet and ran off stage right as the applause faded into nothing. The lights came up. I stood disgraced and breathless as the girl in the wings said, "I was wondering what took you so long. I started to think you were a glory hound." NO! I NEEDED HELP YOU NINNY! What a hilarious and sadly mortifying memory of my Performance Interpreter beginnings. Those were the days. Marilyn, thanks for the competitions. It's where so much of it began for me.

I remember my first date with a Deaf guy... Nope not telling THAT story! Haha! Although, what a story!

I remember advocating for a low-language Deaf girl, as she sat in our ASL classes, trying to apprehend some new knowledge of ASL. The instructor refused to sign and I felt she deserved more than a thoughtless dismissal. I remember how she felt so loved by someone defending and supporting her. She and I became buddies for years. Those were good times.

I remember getting mentored by a woman named Michelle. She was California certified, which as a novice, I considered to be absolutely amazing. She was so good at her job. I would watch her interpret in awe. She gave me incredible feedback, and never made me feel like anything less than a success. She made a tremendous impact on my career. I cherished every semester we had together. Thanks Michelle.

I remember when Gallaudet was Holy Ground, and Deaf people were all Saints.

I remember watching the face of a Deaf kid who had been rejected because of their deafness. I remember a kid wounded when crushed by someone's lack of faith in their abilities. I remember a teen

245

deafened late and struggling with new challenges. I remember having to say, "No" to a Deaf child who wanted to move in with me, because somehow that child felt no acceptance at home, but did with me. I remember the tears they never knew I cried for them.

I remember a beautiful Deaf student in a stunning red dress, standing on a stage at a talent competition. She was so timid and insecure, that is until her song started. I remember the moment she exploded in an indomitable representation of one of the greatest pop stars of all time. I remember seeing the audience stand and scream uncontrollably. I remember when she was finished, thinking, "She will never know how much they loved her." I remember grabbing my team interpreter and the two of us sobbing on each other's shoulders as we saw the undeniable power of what had just happened in the room. She was and is to this day one of the most talented musical interpreters I have ever seen. You still touch my heart girl.

I remember interpreting something "suggestive" at a student meeting, but being so immersed in providing clarity and maintaining the speed of the interpretation that I didn't consider the visual nature of the subject matter, or the fact that 60 teenagers were watching me. I remember suddenly realizing the entire room had become silent. I remember wondering why everyone was staring at me. I remember my very white Deaf student sporting a lovely shade of rose. I remember turning back to the teacher who stood looking at me speechless and thinking "What?" I then clearly remember his words as he turned back to the class and stated, "Gives it a whole new meaning when you see it in sign language, doesn't it?" And then I remembered what I was signing. (Sheepishly...) Oh. It does.

I remember...

– More Thoughts –

Sometimes we get caught up in the daily grind, and we forget the funny, embarrassing, and inspiring moments which led us into this field. We forget the excitement of learning our first signed words. We forget the trepidation of meeting our first Deaf friends. We forget the giddiness of learning new phrases and idioms. We forget the beauty of the language we use. We forget the funny moments along the way and we allow those to give way to so much negativity, frustration and exhaustion. I think we need to stop and remember, and fall in love with sign language and interpreting all over again.

How amazing is this language we use? The creators of ASL were brilliant. Signs like GRACE just amaze me:

- GRACE: *Light from the heavens showering down over us.*

How beautiful is that? There are so many of these beautiful images coming to life in ASL.

- SUPPORT: *A rock moving to position itself under another, offering strength, foundation and support.*
- CONNECT: *A solid but breakable link.*
- EXPRESS: *Everything within you being lifted up and out then offered to others.*

I could go on. There are so many. What an amazing and awe inspiring language. We are so blessed.

I want to encourage you to take a moment and think back to your personal story. Think back to those funny moments which you have allowed to fall away from the forefront of your mind over the years. Go back to the times when you cherished this incredible language, and the Community who gave it to us, and take a moment to smile. Laugh at your mistakes. Acknowledge your progress. Respect the years of effort you have put into the development of your skills. Giggle at unforgettable moments in the Deaf Community. Relive a few of your own stories. Let the beautiful memories fill your hearts. Then... never ever forget.

TERZIS' TIPS!

TAKE TIME FOR YOU!

The cold hard truth is that this job can be all encompassing. We can get so lost in all things "Deaf" that we forget who we are and what we love. Some people are very balanced in this field. I personally don't win any awards for balance. (And everyone who knows me says, "AMEN!") One day, I realized for me to be emotionally and mentally healthy, I needed to do one thing that had no connection with Deafness. I needed a place where I was not an interpreter, not an Executive Director, not a performer, not anything more than just being "Sam". I have chosen different things to hold that sacred position of my "one thing" throughout the years. For six years I volunteered as a Crisis Pregnancy Counselor. I was a Photographer. I was an Orientation Coordinator for a well-known foreign exchange student organization. Until recently, I worked as a Lighting Designer. Most recently, I became the Stage Manager for Star Trek Conventions. Haha! Don't judge me! These have all been things that I loved, and all usually were free of any connection to Deafness. Each have given me time to just be ME!

For some of you it might be horseback riding lessons. For some it could be painting. For others it could be rock climbing. Maybe you should volunteer at a dog shelter. Maybe you would love working at a food pantry. I think interpreters need to find something they love outside of the Deaf World, and do it. Go surfing! Go skiing! Go gator hunting (although personally I think that is insane), just *GO*! Don't go with Deaf people. Don't go with interpreters. Don't bring a business card. Don't prep for the RID on the way there. Just go and be *YOU*. A little *"you time"* can go a long way towards making you a mentally and emotionally healthier and happier individual.

LOOKING AHEAD...

Let's pass on our great passion to future generations of interpreters. Let's leave them with a feeling of awe, the feeling we once had. Let's leave our mark on the Deaf Community and make it a good one. Let's leave the scent of love and acceptance on the field of Interpreting. Let's continue on in our career with a fresh perspective and a new challenge to always grow and do what we do with professionalism and a smile. Let's decide to change ourselves and the world around us for the better. Let's make sure we handle everything from our clothes to our personal responses with professionalism. Let's work as teams and serve each other. Let's accept our humanity yet regularly strive for greatness. Let's make a difference every day. Today is a new day. Smile, my interpreting family! Thanks for joining me on this journey. I look forward to seeing the amazing new memories we will create together...

... and I hope to see you one day at a Star Trek Convention. "Live Long & Prosper."

F.Y.G.L.

Made in the USA
Columbia, SC
10 May 2024

35041483R00147